CORPORATE STRATEGY AND NEW REALITIES

notionpress.com

CORPORATE STRATEGY AND NEW REALITIES

M.Ambashankar
Dean & Director – Academics
Gupta College of Management and Technology
Bangalore

notionpress.com

Notion Press

5 Muthu Kalathy Street, Triplicane,

Chennai - 600 005

First Published by Notion Press 2014

ISBN: 978-93-83808-98-4

INTRODUCTION

For a business to succeed, it is essential for an organization to plan long term, with a firm grasp on its present strengths and weakness. Successful businesses are built on strategies that are built on long-term benefits. Strategic Management is a management activity that involves making decisions based on various analyses and taking relevant actions aimed at achieving long-term competitive advantages.

This book, 'Corporate Strategy and New Realities' is a comprehensive presentation of the subject 'Strategic Management' and covers various aspects of it, such as Strategic Planning, Formulation and Implementation, Business Environment, Organizational Audit and Value, Strategic Options and Models, and finally converting Strategy into Corporate Plans.

This book is presented in a user-friendly and clear, lucid language. Each unit contains an introduction and a list of unit objectives to prepare the student for what to expect in the text. At the end of each unit is a list of key terms and a summary, to aid in recollection. All units contain questions and exercise, and strategically placed 'Check Your Progress' questions so the student can understand and recapitulate what has been learned.

MAPPING IN THE BOOK

Unit 1 - Evolution, Definition, Nature and scope of Strategic Management

Concept of Strategy, evolution, definition, scope and importance of strategy, central concepts in strategic management, collecting information on an external environment, deciding the scope of an organization, acquiring organizational resources and the skills to match the external opportunities and threats, deciding the investment patterns for future, Strategic Management Planning, Scope and importance of Strategic Planning, Strategic decision making, Process of Strategic Management. Levels at which Strategy operates and Roles of Strategists.

Unit II – Strategic Intent

Concept of Strategic Intent, the Mission and Vision, Statements, Defining Mission Statement, Defining A Vision Statement, Creating a sense of Vision, Importance of Vision and Mission Statements, Characteristics and Components of a Mission Statement, Business Definition, Types of Business Activities, objectives of Business.

Strategic Planning Process: Organizational capability, Strategic Advantage, Factors Effecting organizational Capabilities, Functional Capabilities, Marketing Capabilities, Operational Capabilities, Personnel capabilities, Information Management Capability, Factors Effecting organizational Appraisal, approaches to Organizational appraisal, Sources of Information and methods and technique of organizational Appraisal.

Unit III - Business Challenges and Strategic Planning

The Nature and role of Business level Strategies, The Overall Cost Leadership Strategy, The Differentiation Strategy, Location and Time Tactics, Building and Use of Core Competencies,

Building Core Competence, Assessing Core Competence by performing an Internal Audit.

Environmental Appraisal: The Nature of Environment and the Economic Variables, Concept of Environmental Appraisal, Effect of Change in Environment, Need for Environmental Appraisal, Applicability of Environment, Environmental Scanning Techniques, Barriers to Environmental Appraisal, Macro Environment, Auditing Environmental Influences.

Unit IV – Corporate Level Strategies

Concept of Corporate Level Strategies, Corporate Level Strategies in Action, Comparing Business and Military Strategies, Guidelines for Effective Corporate Level Strategies, Grand Strategies, Dimensions to Evaluate Grand Strategies Mix, Types of Strategies, Corporate Restructuring, Mergers, Concept of Synergy.

Strategic Analysis and Choice: Nature of Strategic Analysis and Choice, Process of Generating and Selecting Strategies, Threats – Opportunity – Weakness – Strength (TOWS) Matrix, Boston Consulting Group(BCG) Matrix, GE Nine Cell Matrix, Hofer's Product – Market Evolution Matrix, Shell Directional Policy Matrix, Competitive Analysis: Porter's Five Forces Model, Qualitative Factors in Strategic Choice

Unit V – Strategic Implementation

Nature of Strategy Implementation, Matching Structure with Strategy, Restructuring, Re-engineering, Managing Resistance to Change, Crafting Strategy, Supporting Culture, Production-Operation Concerns when implementing Strategies, Human Resources Concerns when Implementing Strategies, Projects and Procedures, Project Implementation, Procedural Implementation, Resources Allocation, Factors Affecting Resources Allocation; Difficulties in Resource Allocation; Approaches to Resource Allocation, Organizational Structure and Strategic Implementation, Structural Mechanism for Implementation of Strategy; Structures for Strategies.

Unit VI – Strategic Control and Operational Control

Evaluating Strategy Implementation, Evaluating Marketing Issues in Strategy Implementation. Research and Development Issues in Evaluating Strategy Implementation, Evaluating the Importance of Information Systems in Implementing Strategy.

Strategic Control and Operational Control – Strategic Control, Operational Control, Benefits and limitations of Control Techniques, Organizational Systems and Techniques of Strategic Evaluation, Techniques of Strategic Evaluation.

ACKNOWLEDGEMENTS

This book is the product of far more than one brain. I wish to thank many souls who travelled with me in this book journey, but for them this book would not have turned out a quality one. I wish to thank **Mr. B S Gupta** and **Mrs. Indira Gupta** who made me to realize that there is a **Teacher** in me.

I wish to place on record my heartfelt thanks to **Mr.Sudhakara** Principal, and my colleagues at Gupta College.

More than me my 4.00am walking friends **Mr.Nataraj, Prof AVM** and **Mr.Shivaprasad** wanted me to come out with this book because of their earnest interest in me.

Mr. Jayaraj a friend in need and a person of all seasons wanted me to excel at all times. But for him this book would not have seen the daylight, I thank him from bottom of my heart.

Mr. Manjunath H, a friend who always kept a tab on my financial health, wanted me to write not only text books but also my biography, may be his wishes might come true in the near future.

I thank my auditor **Mr. Madhukar Hedge** who always wished that my financials swell proportionately to my qualification, I hope that would happen in near future.

One person who worked more than me for this book is my Executive Assistant **Ms. Deena Mohan**, a wonderful soul and a good human, I thank her whole heartedly.

Finally, I thank **Almighty** who gave me the spirit '**Never Say Die**'

CONTENTS

Unit 1

EVOLUTION OF STRATEGIC PLANNING

INTRODUCTION

Upcoming businessmen often wonder why and how some business perform better than others. Most often, the answer is that successful businesses are built on strategies that result in long-term benefits. Strategic management can therefore be defined as a management activity that involves making decisions based on various analyses and taking relevant action aimed at achieving long-term competitive advantages. The factors to be considered in strategic management are as follows:

1. Organizational goals
2. Stakeholders
3. Short-term and long-term perspectives
4. Effectiveness vs efficiency

Strategy is the channel or direction adopted by an organization with a view to changing its resources in keeping with the changing environment and modifying markets and customers in a manner that will benefit its shareholders. Strategy also implies the path adopted to achieve organizational goals.

UNIT OBJECTIVES

After going through this unit, you will be able to:

- Understand the concept of strategy
- Appreciate the characteristics of strategic decisions
- Differentiate between Operational Efficiency and Strategy

- Get an idea of the evolution of strategic management
- Appreciate the contribution made by strategy gurus
- Understand the various levels of strategic management

CHARACTERISTIC OF STRATEGIC DECISIONS

Strategic decisions are critical to an organization in the long term. Therefore, they have the following essential characteristics:

1. They are concerned with the scope of an organization in the long term
2. They are aimed at achieving an edge over competition.
3. They attempt to ensure that organizational resources and activities are in harmony with the environment they confront.
4. They call for optimum utilization of resources and creation of opportunities.
5. They usually result in resource changes and are complicated in nature.
6. They are often made in uncertain situations.
7. They involve a unified approach to managing the organization.

A set of critical decisions and actions that results n the creation and implementation of strategies aimed at the achievement of organizational goals can be called strategic management. The critical decisions that strategic management encompasses incorporates all aspects of the organization, affecting its performance and existence in the long run; for example, products, resources, organizational structure, etc. The end result of strategic management can be seen in the form of new products, new markets, and adoption of the latest technologies and skills.

Managers are expected to be strategists. They are expected to question the current establishment, structure and set-up and think ahead.

DIFFERENCE BETWEEN OPERATIONAL EFFICIENCY AND STRATEGY

To a layman, a business achieves operational efficiency only when it finds the best way to produce what they want and achieve what they desire. This can only happen when the right people (possessing the relevant skills), the right processes and the latest technology are combined to produce the desired product at minimal cost. Operational strategy, on the other hand is concerned with making decisions that affect the long-term performance of a business. The difference is that while the former is more concerned with the present, the latter is concerned with the future. Excessive attention to the present and neglecting the future can spell disaster for an organization. Therefore, a balance needs to be achieved.

EVOLUTION OF THE CONCEPT OF STRATEGIC MANAGEMENT

The word strategy stems from the Greek word Strategia, which means an army general or a military commander. Battles are fought based on well-conceived strategies. Wars are reinforced by strategies. Similarly, businesses can be referred to as battles based on business strategies. The success of a business or its victory over another in terms of capturing the market share is dependent on its strategy.

In the 1960s, there was little competition for organizations. There were immense opportunities and companies had to merely perform the function of setting long-term goals and their capabilities to meet those goals.

In the 1970s, external influence such as the environment was given more importance while designing strategies. Opportunities and resources became limited and attention was shifted to organizational growth through progressive changes and diversification.

In the 1980s, with emerging competition from the newly industrialized countries, the focus of strategic management and planning shifted to accomplishing and promoting a competitive edge. Business considered mergers and acquisitions to gain advantage to size over competition. Organizations formulated competitive strategies and attempted to provide more value to their customers in order to establish profitable and sustainable positions in their respective industries.

In the 1990s, markets and business became increasingly complicated. This was mainly attributed to advancement in technology, increase in global competition, changing tastes of consumers and fluctuations in exchange rates. Taking on the ever-changing business environment became the main focus of most organizations. Close and continuous monitoring of autonomous and indigenous conditions became definitive to strategic management.

The dynamic business environment of the twenty-first century, continual transformation and new development became the formula for success. With progressing information technology and the advent of globalization, businesses need to be more flexible, need to work on adaptable processes and realize the significance of competitive advantage. It therefore becomes integral to select superior functional strategies that add value to the business, the customers and the stakeholders.

WORK DONE IN THE FIELD OF STRATEGY

The concept of strategy was pioneered by Igor Ansoff and developed further by Henry Mintzberg and Michael Porter.

Ansoff's Strategic Success Paradigm

Igor Ansoff promoted the systematic study of strategic management. During extensive research, he discovered those American businesses that were acquired on the basis of a realistic and far-sighted strategies were more successful than those acquisitions that were done on the basis of immediate or transient benefits. The strategic success paradigm points out the conditions that lead to optimum profits. According to this paradigm:

a) There is no universal formula for success that can be applied to all businesses.

b) Depending on the turbulence in the environment, a business can decide on the degree of aggressiveness of the strategy in order to achieve optimum success.

c) The success strategies for different firms depend on the level of changes, instability or agitation in the environment.

d) The success of a firm depends on the political, psychological, cognitive, anthropological as well as sociological variables. These variables, together, form the internal capability variables.

Based on thorough empirical testing for over a decade, Ansoff translated his success paradigm into a diagnostic instrument, named 'Strategic Readiness Diagnosis'. Ansoff's contribution to the development of the concept of strategic management developed/transformed into books entitled Corporate Strategy and An Analytical Approach to Business Policy for Growth and Expectation. In the former book, published in 1965, he discusses strategic planning whereas in the latter book he introduces the concept of synergy and 'gap analysis'.

Henry Mintzberg: Strategy as a Craft

Henry Mintzberg contributed to the development of strategic management by adding a new dimension to the field. His perceptive view of the field of strategic management incorporated the manager's personal opinion. His view point challenged the views of other rational thinkers of his time. The task of formulating a strategy was considered by him as immensely calculative, critical and sensitive. Propagating a more humane approach to the formulation and implementation of strategies, he came up with the term 'Crafting Strategy' for the same. Accordingly, an ideal organizational structure would be one with (i) a simple organizational structure,

(ii) machine and professional bureaucracy, (iii) adhocracy, and (iv) a divisionalized form.

Peter Drucker's Contribution

Peter Drucker propagated the practice of using formal strategic thinking in management decision after Second World War for a long time; markets were treated as autonomous entities unstrained by organizational checks. However, in these times constituting multidivisional organizations, managing came to mean taking responsibility for attempting to mould the economic environment and conditions are barricading economic shortcomings against the organization's autonomy. Peter Drucker argued that management translated into relevant action aimed to achieve desired results. He was of the opinion that management was much more than passive adaptive behavior.

The concept of management by objectives, popularly known as MBO, was introduced by Drucker in 1954. Before MBO came into existence, managers were more involved with processes than with goals. MBO caused them to shift their concern from processes to goals. Drucker described MBO as not just a management technique but a management philosophy. The basic assumptions of managing were shifted from exercising control to self-control.

Michael Porter: Strategy and Competitive Advantage

Michael Porter recommended the use of his 'Five Forces Model' to study the different elements that comprise strategic management, such as the conditions of company operations. Generic strategic such as Cost Leadership, focus and cost differentiation were introduced by Michael Porter with an aim to decrease the uncertainties of the competitive environment.

Porter authored the following books:

i. Competitive Strategy (1980)

ii. The Competitive Advantage of Nations (1990)

In this book, Porter discusses the issues of sustaining competitive advantage, economic development and competitiveness.

Porter's 'Five Forces Model' states that in any industry, competition is dependent on the following five forces:

i. The threat posed by new entrants

ii. Suppliers' bargaining power

iii. The threat posed by substitute products

iv. The existing rivalry between current products

v. Buyers' or customers 'bargaining power

To survive and succeed in this volatile business environment, it becomes integral for an organization to understand how these five forces operate and influence industry. These forces will be discussed in detail in unit 5.

DIMENSIONS OF STRATEGIC DECISIONS

There are six typical dimensions that are identifiable in strategic issues, which

a) Require decisions to be made by top management

b) Involve the allocation of a large amount of resources of the company

c) Have a significant impact on the prosperity of a firm in the long run

d) Are future- oriented?

e) Have multifunctional

f) Make it necessary to cinder external environmental factors.

LEVELS OF STRATEGIC DECISIONS

The main hierarchical levels of strategy planning are:

a) Corporate level

b) Business level

c) Functional level

A company gets its direction from the managers at the Corporate Level. They act as captains guiding the organization and help it face the challenges of the dynamic business environment. Managers at the Business Level are responsible for shaping the Corporate Managers' vision. At the third or functional level, are managers who transform this vision into reality? The contribution made by manager's at all three levels are important.

Corporate-Level Strategies are aimed at optimum utilization of a company's competencies in the long term. Decisions made by managers at the corporate level incorporate interests of the stakeholders and the society. These strategies mainly concern the choice of operational areas for the company's business. At this level strategies are designed with the objectives of the Organization in mind". These Strategies influence the way business is managed. It also impacts resource management and the manner in which financial resources are invested in various units.

Business-level strategies involve decisions about the competitive edge of a single business unit. At this level, the managers establish functional objectives and individual strategies for business division on the basis of general statements issued by corporate strategic planners. The business-level managers determine the basis of the company's competitive advantage in a particular product or market area. Their goal is to select the most profitable segment and enter it. They also aim to grow in the segment that has the highest potential for growth. In short, this strategy is concerned with using the cost-leadership, differentiation and focus strategies to ensure an edge over competition.

Functional-level strategies constitute short-term strategies with fixed annual objectives in research and development, finance and accounting, marketing, and human resource. Functional-level managers are concerned with problems related to the efficiency and effectiveness of production, success of particular products and services in increasing their market share and quality of customer service. The functional objectives are operational and can be quantified and depending on the operations and requirements of the business, these can be changed or modified. The risk involved in functional strategies is not very high as the cost of failure is small.

Table 1.1 Shows the characteristics of management decisions at different levels.

Table 1.1 Characteristics of Management

	Level of Strategy		
Characteristic	Corporate	Business	Functional
Type	Conceptual	Mixed	Operational
Measurability	Value Adjustments dominate	Semi	Usually quantifiable
Frequency	Periodic or Sporadic	Periodic or sporadic	Periodic
Adaptability	Low	Medium	High
Relation to Present activities	Innovative	Mixed	Supplementary
Risk	Wide range	Moderate	Low
Profit potential	Large	Medium	Small
Cost	Major	Medium	Modest
Time horizon	Long range	Long range	Short range
Flexibility	High	Medium	Low
Cooperation Required	Considerable	Moderate	Little

FROM LONG-RANGE PLANNING TO STRATEGIC PLANNING AND STRATEGIC MANAGEMENT

From the 1950s to the 1970s, the process of planning and implementation using budgets and enforcing capital budgeting and MBOs through control systems, was used for leading a company into the future. However, this was not adequate for highlighting the future goals and issues. This gave birth to long-range planning, which was further replaced by strategic planning and later by strategic management. In recent times, the term strategic management is used to describe the process of strategic decision-making becoming an integral part of the theoretical framework of business policy courses.

SUMMARY

In this unit, you have learned that the long-term direction and scope of an organization is referred to as its strategy. A strategy is aimed at incorporating the firm's resources to altering conditions relating to markets, customers and stakeholders of the organization. You have further been introduced to various characteristics of strategic decisions, which have been defined as a set of critical decisions and actions leading to the formulation and implementation of strategies aimed at achieving organizational goals. The difference between operational efficiency and strategy is that while the former is more concerned with the present, the latter is concerned with the future.

Ansoff promoted the systematic study of strategic management, emphasizing on the benefits of long-term. Henry Mintzberg's perceptive view of the field of strategic management incorporated the manager's personal opinion, propagating a more humane approach to the formulation and implementation of strategies. Peter Drucker introduced the concept of Management by Objectives (MBO), introducing generic strategies including focus, cost leadership and cost differentiation. Porter introduced the 'Five Forces model'.

You have also learned that there are six dimensions of strategic decisions that are operative in establishing a successful business strategy. The main levels of strategic decisions include the corporate level, the business level and the functional level. Corporate-level strategies are aimed at the optimum utilization of a company's competencies in the long term. Business-level strategies involve decisions about the competitive edge of a single business unit and functional-level strategies constitute short-term strategies with fixed annual objectives.

KEY TERMS

- **Strategic management:** A management activity involving decision-making, based on various analyses, and taking relevant action aimed at achieving long-term competitive advantages.
- **Strategy:** A channel or direction that an organization adopts with a view to changing its resources with the changing environment and modifying markets in a manner that will benefit the shareholders.
- **Strategic decisions:** Decisions critical to an organization in the long term.
- **Strategists:** People who question the current establishment, structure and set-up and think with a future vision.
- **Management by Objectives (MBO):** A management philosophy where the focus is on goals rather than processes; self-control rather than external control.

ANWERS TO 'CHECK YOUR PROGRESS'

1. A business achieves operational efficiency only when it finds the best way to produce what they want and achieve what they desire. Operational strategy, on the other hand is concerned with making decisions that affect the long-term performance of the business. The difference being that while the former is more concerned with the present, the latter is concerned with the future.
2. The various characteristics of strategic decisions include:
   a) They are concerned with the scope of an organization in the long term.
   b) They are aimed at achieving an edge over competition.
   c) They attempt to ensure that the organizational resources and activities are in harmony with the environment they confront.
   d) They call for optimum utilization of resources and creation of opportunities.

e) They usually result in resource changes and are complicated in nature.

f) They are often made in uncertain situations.

g) They involve a unified approach to managing the organization.

3. The five forces of Porter's 'Five Forces Model' are:

    a) The threat posed by new entrants

    b) Suppliers' bargaining power

    c) The threat posed by substitute products

    d) The existing rivalry between current players

    e) Buyers' or customers' bargaining power

4. There are six dimensions that are identifiable in strategic issues. These:

    a) Require decisions to be made by the top management

    b) Involve the allocation of a large amount of resources of the company

    c) Have a significant impact on the prosperity of a firm in the long run

    d) Are future-oriented

    e) Have multi-functional or multi-business consequences

    f) Make it necessary to consider the external environmental factors

5. The main levels of strategy planning are:

    a) Corporate level

    b) Business level

    c) Functional level

6. Functional-level managers are concerned with problems related to efficiency and effectiveness of production, success of particular products and services in increasing their market share and quality of customer services.

QUESTIONS AND EXERCIES

Short-Answer Questions

1. Define strategic management.
2. What are the characteristics of a strategic management decision?
3. What are the dimensions of strategic decisions?

Long-Answer Questions

1. Explain the evolution of the strategic management process.
2. Explain the different levels of strategy and illustrate with industry examples.
3. What has been the contribution in this field of renowned management thinkers?

FURTHER READING

Johnson, Gerry and kevan Scholes. 1994. Exploring Corporate Strategy: Text and Cases. New Delhi: Prentice-Hall of India. Thompson, Arthur A. and A. J. Strickland. 1997. Strategic Management: Concepts and Cases. Illinois: Irwin Professional Publishing.

Dess, Gregory G., G.T. Lumpkin and Alan B. Eisner. 2008. Strategic Management: Text and Cases. New York: McGraw-Hill/ Irwin.

Pearce, John A. and Richard B.Robinson. 1999. Strategic Management. New York: McGraw- Hill.

Kazmi, Azhar. 2002. Business Policy and Strategic Management. New Delhi: Tata McGraw-Hill.

Unit 2

STRATEGIC INTENT AND PLANNING PROCESS

INTRODUCTION

Strategic intent is the vision of a company's long-term objectives and goals. The intent gives the company a sense of direction. It also gives employees more chances to explore their potential. This unit discusses the strategic intent and planning process of a company. It covers many topics, such as organizational structure; corporate culture-values, ethics and social responsibility; leadership and its importance; a company's objectives and strategic analysis; and human resource strategy, among other things.

Unit OBJECTIVES

After going through this Unit, you will be able to:

- Explain Strategic intent and implementation
- Understand the components of strategic management
- Describe organizational structure
- Explain organizational culture
- Explain human resource strategy

STRATEGY INTENT AND IMPLEMENTATION

The vision of a company's long-term goals and objectives is referred to as the strategic intent. It is the cornerstone of strategic architecture. While strategic architecture enlightens the future path, it is the strategic intent that provides the emotional and intellectual the future path, it is the strategic intent that provides the emotional and intellectual energy necessary for the journey. Strategic intent involves a significant stretch for the organization as the existing skills, capabilities and resources are not considered sufficient for the task. In traditional organizations, efforts are made to ensure a 'fit' between existing resources and emerging opportunities. In contrast, the concept of strategic intent involves the deliberate creation of a 'misfit' between resources and aspirations.

Strategic intent also envisages the company's position in the long run. Thus, intent conveys a sense of direction. Similarly, strategic intent furthers a unique point of view about the future, giving employees an opportunity to explore something new, enhancing a sense of exploration. Strategic intent instigates an emotional connect and incites a sense of shared destiny. Employees feel that the pursuit of the company's goals is a worthwhile experience.

COMPONENTS OF STRATEGIC MANAGEMENT

While finalizing their business strategy, strategic planners keep in mind certain components of strategic management that help them design effective plans for the future of the company. Some of the important components are as follows:

i. Vision of the company
ii. Mission of the company
iii. Profile of the company
iv. Annual objectives
v. External environment
vi. Strategic analysis and choice
vii. Long-term objectives
viii. Grand strategy
ix. Functional and operational strategies
x. Company's policies
xi. Control and evaluation

Vision

Organizations generally describe their goals and intentions in a broad category. This description depicts the company's aims as well as future prospects, providing a vantage point for an organization's future direction and course of business activity. It is often communicated through the mission statement. Above all, vision is a powerful motivator and keeps an organization moving forward in the intended direction. Although, to a layman, the vision and the mission of a company may seem overlapping or similar, the fact is that the vision of a company is not always as specific as the mission statement. Usually, the vision is impersonal a not even written down.

Let us look at the company vision of a Zydus Cadila Group. Before you understand the vision of the Group, here is the profile of the company in brief. The main activity of the group – Cadila Healthcare Ltd, founded in 1952-is to come up with healthcare solutions. They produce active pharmaceutical ingredients, cosmeceuticals, herbal products, vaccines, etc. The group has plants in Navi Mumbai, Patalganga, Vadodara, Ahmedabad, Andheri, Goa and Ankleshwar. In 1955, the group came to be known as the Zydus Cadila Group following restructuring. Cadila Healthcare is the Group's flagship company that introduced an IPO in February 2000. The Zydus Group is not only aiming to be a global player but is also pursuing an ambition of becoming one of the top three healthcare companies in India. The Group has already made its presence felt in the markets of the US, EU, Brazil, South Africa and Algeria.

Their vision is stated as follows:

'Zydus shall be a leading healthcare provider with a robust product pipeline and sales of over $1 billion by 2010. We shall achieve sales of over $ 3 billion by 2015 and be a research-based pharmaceutical company by 2020.'

Source: http://www.nutralite.com/about_us.htm

Company Mission

The mission of a company is very important in a company's successful performance not only in the short run, but also in the long run. The mission of a company is not vague as the vision and is designed to ensure that those belonging to the company work together with a uniform purpose. It is slightly more specific and sets apart one company from the other companies in the same area of business. The mission identifies the scope of the company's operations, describes the company's product, market and technological areas of thrust, and reflects the values and priorities of its strategic decision makers. The mission of a business looks towards an endless future as if the firm were immortal. It reflects the intentions that a company hopes to realize some time in the future. The mission statement is formulated as if the firm were immortal. It reflects the intentions that a company hopes to realize some time in the future. The mission statement is formulated after much thought and with great caution keeping in mind the basic product of the company, the market it operates in, the technology used, the image of the company as well as its goals and philosophy. However, despite being more specific than the vision, the mission of the company may not provide specific directions or channels for action or achievement of goals. The mission statement of a company often reflects social responsibility and addresses issues that concern not just its own employees, customers and shareholders but the local community and the society in general. While formulating the mission statement, the ethics and norms to be followed with respect to the general public and the industry as a whole are also kept in mind. To give you a clear idea, here are a few examples.

i. Cadila Healthcare, a company that has been discussed in the previous paragraph, states its company mission as follows:

   'We are dedicated to life... in all its dimensions. Our world is shaped by a passion for innovation, commitment to partners and concern for people in an effort to create healthier communities, globally.'

Source: http://www.nutralite.com/about_us.htm

ii. Unilever is a company with almost four hundred well-known brands spanning almost fourteen categories of food, personal grooming and home products. Its most popular brands include Axe, Lux and Knorr. The Company's mission reads something like this

'Unilever's mission is to add vitality to life. We meet everyday's need for nutrition, hygiene, and personal care with brands that help people feel good, look good and get more out of life.'

Source:

http://www.unilever.com/ourcompany/aboutunilever

iii. You can get an idea of Hindustan Unilever's mission from the following lines:

'HUL believes that to succeed requires the highest stands of corporate behavior towards our employees, consumers and the societies and world in which we live.'

Source: http://hul.co.in/index.htm

Company Profile

The profile of a company depicts the quantity and quality of the company's financial, human and physical resources. The profile assesses the strengths and weaknesses of the company's management and organizational structure. It also analyses the company's past success and traditional concerns in the context of the company's current capabilities, in an attempt to identify its future capabilities. A look at the various corporate websites on the Internet will give you a very good idea of how a company's profile is presented to the outside world.

External Environment

All those forces that affect the organization from the outside or all the conditions that effect an organization's strategic options and define its competitive situation, are referred to as its external environment. It consists of three interactive segments, namely the operating environment, the industry environment and the remote environment.

Strategic Analysis and Choice

Strategic analysis enables a firm to identify a range of possible attractive investment opportunities. Opportunities that are compatible with the company's mission are identified as desired opportunities. If the list of desired opportunities is further weeded out, the potential options or strategic choices can be identified. The entire process of strategic choice is meant to combine long-term objectives and generic and grand strategies in order to place the firm in an optimal position in the external environment for achievement of the company mission.

Strategic analysis and strategic choice in a single or dominant product business involve the identification of strategies that are most effective at building a sustainable competitive advantage. Such a competitive advantage is based on key value chain activities and capabilities, i.e., the core competencies of a firm. Multi business organizations focus on the best combination of businesses to maximize their shareholder value.

Objectives: Annual, Short-Term and Long-Term

Objectives refer to the purpose behind an action or activity. As the name suggests, annual objectives are the objectives that a firm aims to achieve in one year. Objectives can be both short-term as well as long-term and belong to the same areas of business. However, the only difference is that the short-term objectives are more specific as they need to be achieved in a short span of time. In fact, the short-term objectives are formed on the basis of the long-term objectives. If a firm's long-term objectives are to reduce production costs by 20 per cent within the next five years, then the annual objective could be to reduce its manufacturing costs by 5 per cent every year. Therefore, by achieving its short-term objective, the firm will get close to its long-term objective.

Take a look at the following extract from PepsiCo's website which gives us a rough idea of what the company is committed to and what its vision, mission and objectives are.

PepsiCo's Commitment: Our commitment is to deliver sustained growth, through empowered people, acting with responsibility and building trust. Here's what this means:

Sustained Growth is fundamental to motivating and measuring our success. Our quest for sustained growth stimulates innovation, places a value on results, and helps us understand whether today's actions will contribute to our future. It is about growth of people and company performance. It prioritizes making a difference and getting things done.

Empowered People: Means we have the freedom to act and think in ways that we feel will get the job done, while being consistent with processes that ensure proper governance and being mindful of the rest of the company's needs.

Responsibility and Trust: Forms the foundation for healthy growth. It's about earning the confidence that other people place in us as individuals and as a company. Our responsibility means we take personal and corporate ownership for all we do, to be good stewards of the resources entrusted to us. We build trust between ourselves and others by walking the talk and being committed to succeeding together.

PepsiCo's Guiding Principles

This is how we carry out our commitment.

We must always strive to:

Care for customers, consumers and the world we live in. We are driven by an intense, competitive spirit in the marketplace, but we direct this spirit toward solutions that achieve a win for each of our constituents as well as a win for the corporation. Our success depends on a thorough understanding of our customers, consumers and communities. Caring, means going the extra mile. Essentially, this is a spirit of growing rather than taking.

Sell only products we can be proud of. The test of our standards is that we must be able to personally endorse our products without reservation and consume them ourselves. This principle extends to every part of the business, from the purchasing of ingredients to the point where our products reach the consumer's hands.

Speak with truth and candor. We speak up, telling the whole picture, not just what is convenient to achieving individual goals. In addition to being clear, honest and accurate, we take responsibility to ensure our communications are understood.

Balance short term and long term. We make decisions that hold both short-term and long-term risks and benefits in balance over time. Without this balance, we cannot achieve the goal of sustainable growth.

Win with diversity and inclusion. We leverage a work environment that embraces people with diverse backgrounds, traits and different ways of thinking. This leads to innovation, the ability to identify new market opportunities, all of which helps develop new products and drives our ability to sustain our commitments to growth through empowered people.

Respect other and succeed together. This company is built on individual excellence and personal accountability, but no one can achieve our goal by acting alone. We need great people who also have the capability of working together, whether in structured teams or informal collaboration. Mutual success is absolutely dependent on treating everyone who touches the business with respect, inside and outside the company. A spirit of fun, our respect for others and the value we put on teamwork make us a company people enjoy being part of, and this enables us to deliver world-class performance.

Source:

http://www.pepsico.com/PEP_Citizenship/pepsicoValues/index.cfm

Projects and Procedural Issues

The process of strategy formulation is referred to in current literature as 'strategic planning' and is distinguished from 'Management Planning/and Control' for strategy implementation. Strategic planning incorporates an organizations objective, the variation in the objectives, the means to acquire them and the technique that analyses the entire process. Sources: projects. Ics.hawaii.edu

The procedural issues are associated with the ongoing administration of an enterprise. It is the process by which managers assure that resources are obtained and used effectively and efficiently in the accomplishment of organization's objectives.

The management planning system involves the preparation of annual plans based on the overall corporate goals and objectives in terms of sales, costs, margins, profits and returns of sales, costs, margins, profits and return on capital, branched as necessary, in relation to products, operations, and geographic location of activities.

An effective planning and control system requires the organization structure to be such that it defines authority and responsibility in terms of tasks to be accomplished.

For effective implementation of strategy, the essential elements of the planning and control system should consist of:

i. An appropriate organizational structure that defines authority and responsibility, in terms of the task to be accomplished

ii. Goals and targets of organizational units based on the input-output relationship in the relevant operations.

iii. A reporting system that can quickly diagnose deviations from the desired results, particularly in those areas which represent key variables in operations

iv. A follow up mechanism to ensure prompt remedial action by proper analysis, review and coordinated action.

v. Participation and support of all levels of management and supervisory personnel.

ORGANIZATIONAL STRUCTURE

The detailed purpose of strategic management is enumerated in the following table:

Strategic position	Scanning the external environment Meeting stakeholder's expectations Utilizing resources and competencies
Strategic choice	Identifying alternative strategies Evaluating the alternatives Selecting the strategies
Implementation of Strategy	Modifying the organization structure and design Planning and allocating resources Managing strategic change

Strategic Position:

The strategic position of a company is determined by the influences that the changes in the external environment may have. The strategic position is affected by the advantages that the resources within the organization may have, or the opportunities they may give rise to. It is also affected by the wants and expectations of the stakeholders, managers, shareholders and unions associated with the organization.

Scanning the external environment

The organization exists and functions in an environment that is far from simple. It exists in a continuously changing environment wrought with legal, technological, commercial, social as well as political complexities. These complexities impact some businesses more than others and that too in different ways. In some cases, these changes may lead to opportunities whereas in other cases, these may threaten the very existence of an organization.

Utilizing resources and competencies

The Strategic capabilities of an organization largely depend on its competencies and internal resources. These form the internal influences. The organization should be able to identify the factors that are hindering the future strategic choices in order to deal with them accordingly. Some resources such as the core competencies may give rise to competitive advantages. The core competencies generally deal with skills, knowledge and activities.

Meeting stakeholders' expectations

The organization is influenced by a number of factors including the stakeholders" expectations. Some strategies designed by the management may not be approved by the stakeholders. If the stakeholders are more powerful, they will influence the management's strategy and even modify it to suit them. In case the management is more powerful, their strategy will ultimately be accepted by one and all. Another factor that influences the organization strategy is the culture followed within the organization as well as by the world outside. The strategic position of an organization can be evaluated and determined by the combined influence of its own capability as well as the political, social and cultural environment within and outside.

Strategic Choice

In order to make strategic choices, you have to first understand the corporate-level factors as well as the business unit-level factors that form the foundation of the strategic choices for the future. You also have to get an idea of the available options for developing strategies, that is, the technique to be followed and the channel or path to be adopted. As already discussed in the previous unit, strategies are formed at various levels. At the corporate level, that is, the highest level, the strategy formulation mainly takes into consideration the various business units and how they can be improved with active contribution from the corporate centre. It is but natural that the small business units look up the corporate centre as a parent for all their needs-channelizing the resources in the right direction, allocating finances appropriately, building brand image as well as marketing their products or services. Strategic choices at this level are made to provide the organization with a competitive edge based on a thorough study of the market and customers' demands and expectations.

Implementation of Strategy

Putting the selected strategies into action is concerned with ensuring that the structure and design of the organization are conducive to implementation; the resources are planned, managed and allocated in the manner favorable to implementation; the processes are designed in a suitable manner; the relationship between the departments and units facilitates productivity, performance and action.

Once the organization is structured and designed suitably, the next step is to plan and allocate the limited resources available to facilitate strategy implementation and ensure optimum utilization with optimum profit. At the same time, the planning and allocation should adjust with the demands of the external environment in order to provide a competitive advantage.

Finally, strategy implementation also involves effective restructuring and reengineering, that is, effective management of strategic change. Examples of managing strategic change involve how successfully an organization takes care of a restructuring or reengineering exercise carried out in the company and the fallout of the same. It can also involve how an acquisition process is integrated with the acquiring company.

CORPORATE CULTURE –VALUES, ETHICS AND SOCIAL RESPONSIBILITY

In today's world, the need for leadership is primary, but how do we go about encouraging it? Let us focus on business organizations. It is essential to enforce development and progress. Custodial management does not imply leadership. Leadership is in keeping with the leader's objectives, aiming at specific objectives and their implementation. The definition implies dissatisfaction with the conventional pertaining to a transformative process aimed at well-defined objectives.

Leadership: Three Interdependent Activities

Richard D' Aveni, author of Hyper Competition, argued that in a world where all dimensions of competition appear to be compressed in time and heightened in complexity, sustainable competitive advantages are no longer possible.

Leaders are thus change agents whose success is measured by their efficiency in implementing a strategic vision.

Accordingly, many authors contend that successful leaders must recognize three independent activities that must be continually reassessed for organizations to succeed. These are:

i. Determining a direction

ii. Designing the organization

iii. Nurturing a culture dedicated to excellence and ethical behavior

The interdependent nature of these three activities is self-evident. Consider, an organization with a great mission and a superb organizational structure and design, but a culture that implicitly encourages shirking and unethical behavior; or a strong culture and organization design but little direction and vision; or one with a sound direction and strong culture but counterproductive teams and a zero-sum reward system, that leads to the dysfunctional situation in which one party's gain is viewed as another party's loss, and collaboration and sharing are severely hampered.

Much of the failure of today's organizations can be attributed to a lack of consideration of these three activities. Let us have a look at the three interdependent activities.

Determining the direction

Leaders need a holistic understanding of an organization's stakeholders, which requires an ability to examine the environment in order to develop knowledge of all the company's stakeholders (e.g., customers, suppliers, shareholders) and other conditions, which help to overcome obstacles and develop a beneficial strategic approach, forming a framework of the basic objectives, promoting employee involvement marking future organizational goals.

Designing the organization

At times, almost all leaders have difficulty implementing their vision and strategies. Such problems stem from a variety of sources, including:

- Lack of coordination among managers
- Uninspiring incentives hampering the organization's objectives

- Insubstantial budgeting and control systems
- Failure of coordination across the organization

Successful leaders are actively involved in building structures, teams, systems and organizational processes that facilitate the implementation of their vision and strategies.

A firm would generally be unable to attain an overall cost-leadership without closely monitoring its costs through detailed and formalized cost and financial control procedures. In a similar vein, achieving a differentiation advantage would necessitate encouraging innovation, creativity and sensitivity to market conditions. Such efforts would be typically impeded by the use of a huge set of cumbersome rules and regulations, as well as highly centralized decision-making. With regard to corporate level strategy, a related diversification strategy would necessitate reward systems that emphasize behavioral measures to promote sharing across divisions within a firm. However, an unrelated strategy should rely more on financial indicators of performance, such as revenue gains and profitability, since there is less need for collaboration across business units due to lack of uniformity.

Nurturing a culture dedicated to excellence and ethical behavior

Organizational culture can be an effective and positive means of organizational control. Leaders play a pivotal role in developing and sustaining as well as changing when necessary, an organization's culture.

Clearly, a leader's ethical behavior can make a strong impact on an organization-for good or for bad. The top executives and managing directors are responsible for establishing a uniform ethical norm across the organization, representing the organizational objectives. Several elements must be present and reinforced for a firm to become a highly ethical organization role models, corporate credos and codes of conduct, reward and evaluation systems, and policies as well as procedures.

Overcoming Barriers to Change and Effective Use of Power

Recipe for success

The following is a study of the working culture at Kao Corporation, Japan

Creating a sense of stretch- An important characteristic exhibited by Kao Corporation, stretch is not just about top management redefining its strategic vision in more grandiose terms or substituting seemingly impossible targets for the usual budget objectives. Workers at mid-level and frontline operations should be made to view themselves and the organization with a future vision.

However, liberating the organization from the restrictive patterns of the past and increasing the employee's expectations is not easy. But Kao was able to do so by building the following characteristics into its culture:

i. A shared responsibility

ii. A collective identity

iii. Personal commitment

i. Building a shared responsibility – Few people want to work for an organization that aspires to be average. It is part of human nature to want to excel, to be part of a winning team. Although all good managers recognize this simple truth, surprisingly few have been able to respond to the need it creates within their own organization. The problem has usually been that they have tried to engage their employees intellectually, through rational strategic analysis rather than emotionally through the allure of bold ambition. At the broadest level, this can be an overarching ambition that gives more personal meaning to the company's long term objectives. For Kao such a shared ambition was instilled into the organization by Dr. Maruta from the moment he became president in 1971, till his retirement in 1994. Maruta wanted every employee to understand that Kao was obliged to develop its technologies and apply them in innovative ways. He established within the organization a winning ambition to create a broad portfolio of products that were useful to society and offered good value to consumers. Kao's statement of purposeful ambition was in sharp contrast to the banality of so many other companies superficial mission statements printed in annual reports and then ignored completely. Within Kao the creation of useful new products became the driving force behind all activities.

ii. Developing a collective identity - Setting one's sights on highly ambitious objectives can be an intimidating prospect for many companies and people, since the bolder and more aggressive the goals, the greater the likelihood of their failure. Yet, acting in concert with others, most individuals develop a sense of courage and commitment they are unable to muster on their own. This is the potential that we saw various companies capture as they generated a sense of collective identity around the ambitious targets of becoming the best they could get. Kao's open and mutually supportive learning environment, framed by Maruta's concept of the company as an educational institution, created just such a collective commitment to the company's technology and new product development ambitions.

iii. Creating personal commitment – Involving the people in every aspect of the company's business so that they feel sense of personal commitment towards achieving the company's mission can be seen as common thing in Kao. In Kao, literally every employee was involved in the decision making process of the company. The employees were encouraged to give their views on various aspects. (Source: iitk.ac.in)

What are the barriers to change that leaders often encounter, and how can they use power to bring about meaningful change in their organizations? After all, people generally have some level of choice about how strongly they support or resist a leader's change initiates. There are various reasons why organizations and managers are often in defiance to transition:

1. Personal interests nested in the present state of affairs
2. Systemic barriers
3. Behavioral barriers are associated with the tendency of managers to be inclined towards certain issues.
4. Political barriers refer to conflicts arising from power relationships
5. Personal time constraints

Successful leadership requires effective use of power in overcoming barriers to changes. Power refers to a leader's ability to get things done in way a he or she wants them to be achieved. It is the ability to influence other people's behavior, to persuade them to do things that they otherwise would not do, and to overcome resistance and opposition to changing direction. Effective exercise of power is essential focuses for successful leadership.

A leader derives his or her power from several sources or basis. The simplest way to understand the bases of power is by classifying them, as organizational and personal.

Organizational bases of power refer to the power that a person wields because of holding a good management position. These include legitimate power, reward power, coercive power and information power. Legitimate power is derived from organizationally conferred decision-making authority and is exercised by a manager's position in the organization. Reward power depends on the ability of the leader or manager to confer rewards for positive behaviors or outcomes. Coercive power is the power a manager exercises over employees using fear of punishment for errors of omission and commission. Information power arises from a manager's access, control and distribution of information that is not freely available to everyone in an organization.

Apart from organizationally derived power, a leader might be able to influence subordinates because of his or her personality characteristics and behavior. These would be considered as the personal bases of power. The personal bases of power are referent power and expert power. The source of referent power involves a subordinate's identification with the leader. A leader's personal attributes might influence subordinates and make them devoted to that leader. On the other hand, the source of expert power is the leader's expertise and knowledge in a particular field. The leader is the expert on whom subordinates depend for information that facilitates success in operations.

Emotional Intelligence: A Key Leadership Trait

A Vast amount of literature is available on the successful traits of leaders, including business leaders at the highest level.

For simplicity, these traits may be grouped into three broad sets of capabilities:

- Purely technical skills (like accounting and operations research)
- Cognitive abilities (like analytical reasoning or quantitative analysis)
- Emotional intelligence (such as the ability to work with others and passion for work)

One attribute of successful leaders that has become popular in both the literature and management practice in recent years is 'emotional intelligence'. Two of Daniel Goleman's recent books, Emotional Intelligence and Working with Emotional Intelligence were both on the New York Times' best-seller lists. Goleman defines emotional intelligence (EI) as the capacity for recognizing one's own emotions and those of others.

Recent studies of successful managers have found that effective leader's portray a constant emotional intelligence. Findings indicate, for example, EI is proportional to success in life (economic well-being, satisfaction with life, friendship, family life), including, occupational attainments, than IQ. Such evidence has been extrapolated to the catchy phrases; 'IQ gets you hired, but EQ (emotional quotient) gets you promoted.' And surveys show that human resource managers believe this statement to be true, and perhaps even for highly technical jobs such as those of scientists and engineers.

Without EQ, Goleman has argued, a manager can have excellent training, an incisive analytical mind, and many ideas but will still not be a great leader.

There are five components of EI: Self-awareness, Self-regulation, Motivations, Empathy, and Social skill.

Value Creation and Role of Strategic Leadership

Strategic Leadership is highlighted in terms of managerial leadership. Most organizations provide managerial training to executives for leadership which is process based emphasizing specific functions and their passive influence in the process of decision making.

- Events take place more rapidly than ever; most of them are bringing about irreversible changes. Old order of things, products, processes and systems are continuously being destroyed and replaced by technologically superior, faster and smarter ones.
- Knowledge work and knowledge-workers are becoming increasingly the order of the day. Products and processes are becoming technology-driven and hence smarter. This is pressurizing people to become continuously smarter.
- Intellectual assets and their ownership have begun to replace physical assets and their ownership as the primary basis of economic wealth creation and competitive advantage.
- The new era is ushering in tremendous growth opportunities. It is driven by technology, innovation, enterprise, etc. The era has marked the death of permanency: life-cycles are becoming shorter.
- Managing in such situations requires a new competitive mindset-mental agility, organizational flexibility, speed, innovation, global view, strategic thinking etc.

How do we carry our organizations into this cataclysmic, turbulent era? How do we ensure their long-term sustainability? How do we sustain their strategic competitiveness over the coming years?

This is the context of exploring the contours of Strategic Leadership, in clear contrast to the conventional leadership, as the critical resource to steer the organizations into a new era.

What is Strategic Leadership?

Strategic Leadership is found at the executive level of an organization and works in relation to the organization as a whole in contrast to leadership which operates uniformly at all levels. Strategic Leadership can be defined as the leader's ability to anticipate, envision, and maintain flexibility, to think strategically and to work with the members of the team to initiate changes that will create a viable future for the organization. The leader enables the organization to acquire decisive skills, enhancing growth and financial stability.

Two perspectives on Strategic Leadership

There are different perspectives on Strategic Leadership. One of these perceives that organizations are reflections or extended shadows of their founding fathers and later on their chief executives. In this perspective, top managers are armed with substantial decision-making responsibilities and capabilities and they have the ability to significantly influence the direction of the firm and the firm's strategic management process. The top management has the sole influence on the people within the organization and their behavior towards the organizational goals. The CEO, under this perspective, would be a titan full of strategic wisdom, initiative, innovation etc. Given this role and responsibility, he could turn out to be a lone ranger out of touch and out of sync with the people under his leadership. There is an element of great risk when the organization lands up with a CEO who does not fit this perspective of the role, because the people below are ill-equipped and ill-trained to contribute to the noble task of leading and directing the organization. This perspective is fine when the strategic environment in which the organization has to function is reasonable predictable. In a situation that is dynamic and influenced by a multiplicity of forces that are fairly unpredictable it is too much to expect that the top management has all the decision-making capabilities, all the abilities to influence the direction of the firm and to lead the people towards the goals.

The great group's perspective of Strategic Leadership

Under this perspective the organization is perceived not as a piece of property by its current set of shareholders but as a community of people involved in the organization and this community remains together to pursue the common purpose. In any community, each member has something to contribute towards the common purpose; each is inter-dependent on the other. This leads to leadership being 'distributed among diverse individuals who have the responsibility to create a viable future for the organization'. This would lead to the emergence of a variety of networks within the organization. Innovations are created with help from one another; knowledge creation takes place across the organization and it gets dispersed very easily. Strategic thinking and innovation also happen across the organization. There is a higher sense of involvement and ownership and it is a lot easier to bring about any major change in the organization and its processes. These great groups have some interesting characteristics:

i. The members of the groups have accepted their responsibilities and are highly committed to the organizational goals.

ii. The groups learn from a variety of functions and parties including those from outside the firm like suppliers, customers, etc.

iii. The groups have a commitment to information and knowledge as well as their compilation. There is a definite urge to work smarter through collective insights and competencies. One of the important greater groups in any firm is the top management team (TMT) created by the CEO. This is generally a small but core team comprising senior executives from heterogeneous functions and competencies. This team has great potential in providing the Strategic Leadership to the firm. The great groups' perspective does not rule out the need for highly competent top manager/s.

The role of the top managers is to facilitate the development of great groups where Strategic Leadership gets distributed among a variety of people with different competencies. These groups with facilitation from the top managers develop adaptive solutions to the problems that emerge from time to time. The CEO is accountable to the Board of Directors for the firm's performance.

Managerial leadership is impersonal in comparison to strategical leadership. Managers can manage an organization, sustain normal growth rates; but they are less equipped to propel supernormal growth; they are less suited to facilitate innovations and changes. They do not belong or exist in the present; they belong to the future. They are not constrained by the present structure or systems or process or people; they do not draw their sustenance from the present. Visionary leaders are more proactive, creative, innovative and idea generators. They influence the thinking process of the organization and its people. They create fresh approaches to long-standing problems and generate lot of excitement in the organization. Since they are last rooted in the existing structures and systems, they are very often on a plane of high risk and seek out ventures characterized by high-risk-high-returns. They are least systematic as they relate to ideas and people intuitively, emotionally and empathetically. Visionary leaders are good at creating new ideas and grandiose visions for the organization; but they are very weak when it comes to executing or realizing those dreams. A Strategic Leader is a synergistic combination of the 'managerial leader' and the 'visionary leader'.

Strategic Leadership presumes that the leader understands the emergent competitive environment and is able to create strategic directions for organizational excellence. It also presumes that the leader is able to create, nurture and sustain organizational competencies to translate and implement the strategic directions into tangible organizational outcomes. The strategic leader needs to be as maverick as the visionary leader and as stoic and matter-of-fact as the managerial leader. Visionary leadership focuses on the long-term perspective and long-term viability of the organization; managerial leadership focuses on the short-term viability of the organization. He needs to balance between the future and the present; this appears to be contradictory in nature as the expectations and competencies are quite different. This is the paradox of leading and managing.

A successful leader would allow managerial leaders flourish in the organization to take care of day-to-day matters. At the same time, he would let visionary leaders flourish to create strategic options for the future.

Leading and managing

A strategic leader would lead the organization into the future and change; simultaneously he would manage it for its short-term viability. This is a very challenging task. Some leaders achieve this by nurturing separate groups of people with responsibilities to manage long-term perspectives of the firm and to manage the day-to-day affairs of the company. The attitude and skills required for two tasks are different and hence it would be a lot easier to identify separate set of people for the two tasks.

A strategic leader

What factors support the nurturance of Strategic Leadership? It is generally observed that a liberal organizational culture and flexible structure are more likely to support the emergence of Strategic Leadership than a rigid, hierarchical structure with too much emphasis on current performance. When there is too much focus on current operations and profits, there is hardly any scope for vision. This leads to a situation of managerial leadership only. When the organization is too hierarchical and rigid, there is very little scope for innovation, creativity or change. This also prohibits the nurturance of Strategic Leadership. There can also be a situation where the CEO does not encourage creativity, innovation or change leading to a situation where emergence of Strategic Leadership is stifled or discouraged.

In widely diversified organizations, it is found that executive development tends to focus on managerial leadership. The attempt is to develop managers who can manage the business of the firm, whether it is steel making or shipping, with equal comfort and ease. There is a strong possibility that in such situations the process of visioning gets de-emphasized leading to precluding the development of Strategic Leadership in the long run. This is the situation of loss of strategic control

Government is another type of organization where the long-term view is at a discount. This is for a variety of reasons. It could be that the focus is on performance for the immediate or current term of the government with little or no focus on the time horizon beyond the current term. There can be a situation where the objective of the organization is not adequately translated into operational parameters. In government, the output is mostly of social nature; very often there is inadequate efforts in correctly valuing them in financial terms resulting in obfuscation of the focus and hence loss of strategic control.

Among small and medium firms, the inability to grow and to a large extent bankruptcies can also significantly attribute to the absence of Strategic Leadership. For a variety of reasons there is too much of focus on the management of day-to-day affairs, which is managerial leadership. There is conspicuous lack of vision either due to ignorance or due to excessive preoccupation with the present or due to lack of resources. These combine with imperfect capital structures, poor use of external resources and advisors, inadequate emphasis on succession planning and poor management skills. On careful analysis, the prime cause invariably emerges to be the lack of vision and Strategic Leadership.

Developing a Learning Organization

The implicit message is that learning, information sharing, adaptation, decision making and so on are not shared throughout an organization. In contrast, leading-edge organizations recognize the importance of having everyone in the process of actively and adapting.

In today's progressive and ever changing world it becomes intrinsic for an integrated approach at various levels of organizations. 'The person who figures out how to harness the collective genius of the people in his or her organization', is according to former Citibank CEO Walter Wriston, 'is going to below the competition away'.

Successful learning organizations create a proactive, creative approach to the unknown, actively solicit the involvement of employees at all levels, and enable all employees to use their intelligence and apply their imagination. Higher levels skills are required of everyone, not just those at the top. A learning environment involves organization-wide commitment to change an action orientation, and applicable tools and methods. It must be viewed by everyone as a guiding philosophy and not simply as another change programme.

A critical requirement of all learning organizations is that everyone feels and supports a compelling purpose. Inspiring and motivating people with a mission or purpose is a necessary but sufficient condition for developing an organization that can learn and adapt to a rapidly changing, complex and interconnected environment. There are four critical ongoing processes of learning organizations:

- Empowering employees at all levels
- Accumulating and sharing internal knowledge
- Gathering and integrating external information
- Challenging the status quo and encouraging creativity

Strategy Spotlight

Under the direction of Dr.Yoshio Maruta, the then president of Kao Corporation, Kao became one of the most admired companies in Japan regularly rated by Nikkei Business ahead of well-known companies like Canon and Toyota in terms of corporate originality, innovativeness and creativity.

Many of the company's innovativeness in the field of super concentrated detergents and shaped diapers were benchmarks in its field, when compared to its much mightier rivals like P&G and Unilever. It consistently came up with new products ahead of its local competitors such as Lion to emerge as the largest branded and packaged goods company in Japan and second largest in terms cosmetics.

It received the Nikkei Monozukuri Award in November 2006 for promoting product development and manufacturing capabilities. The award is given to outstanding companies for research centers and systems in Japan and overseas. Women's Wear Daily, a fashion magazine, awarded it the breakthrough product of the year 2006 in USA for its Luminous Colour glaze sold under the John Frieda brand in the United States.

The Kao Way- Building the Foundation

The Kao serves as the core index of its business to pursue the mission, 'to strive for the wholehearted satisfaction and enrichment of the lives of people globally.'

In line with its mission the company strives to work with passion in the core domains of cleanliness, beauty, health and chemicals to provide products and brands of excellent value created from the customer's perspective.

The company is truly driven by the values of innovation and integrity and the principles of consumer driven, respect and team work and global perspective.

Founded in 1887 in Japan, the Kao Company was built on the basis of a simple strategy; produce soaps of equal quality to imported brands but at more affordable prices. The management and the employees of Kao soap company believed strongly in the rather grand motto they developed for their tiny company, 'Cleanliness is the foundation of a prosperous society.' For over half a century the company grew, improving its products and building its distribution. Then, in the immediate post war era, following an explicit policy of imitating and adapting foreign technology and marketing approaches, Kao launched the first Japanese laundry detergent. In following years the company expanded into dishwashing detergents and household cleaners, establishing itself as one of the three major Japanese companies that dominated the domestic household cleaning market.

It was not until the 1970s and 1980s that Kao began to pull ahead of its competitors and inflict some humiliating market defeats on the newly arrived foreign players Unilever and Procter and Gamble. It was in this era under the two decade leadership of Dr Yashiro Maruta that Kao developed a management philosophy and organizational capability that wove continuous renewal into the fabric of the company's ongoing activities.

When he assumed the presidency of Kao in 1971, Maruta brought with him a management approach that reflected his deep involvement in Buddhist philosophy. His beliefs were based on the principles of human equality that was expressed as a profound respect for the individual. The philosophy manifests itself in a commitment not only to give employees their own voice but to help them achieve their potential.

Starting from this philosophy introduced a radical concept. He insisted that his managers view Kao not as a soap and detergent company but as an educational institution. He convinced them that the most basic responsibility of every member of the organization was to teach and to learn. As he created his learning organization, Maruta developed sophisticated information systems that allowed managers to capture and process vast amounts of data, adding value and transforming it into usable knowledge. The traditional focus of Kao was shifted from adaptation to creativity and innovation. Maruta also insisted that knowledge building and the learning focus on the future rather than reflect on the past. In order to avoid complacency he discouraged his managers from talking about past achievements.

Creating an Ethical Organization

What is ethics? Ethics may be defined as a system of right or wrong. Ethics assists individuals in deciding when an act is moral or immoral, socially desirable or not. There are many sources for an individuals' ethics. These include religious beliefs, national and ethnic heritage, family practices, community standards and expectations, educational experiences, and friends and neighbors. Business ethics is the application of ethical standards to commercial enterprise.

Individual ethics vs organizational ethics

Many leaders may think of ethics as a question of personal scruples, a confidential matter between employees and their consciences. Such leaders are quick to describe a wrongdoing as an isolated incident, the work of a rogue employee. They assume the company should not bear any responsibility for an individual's misdeeds-it may not even enter their minds. After all, in their view, ethics has nothing to do with leadership.

Ethics is in coalescing with leadership. Individual traits cannot explain the entire corporate behavioral pattern. Unethical behavior patterns incorporate the character patterns of people in an organization, who if not directly then indirectly participate in unethical business practices. Thus, ethics is not limited to personal behavior patterns but it constitutes the entire organizations behavioral norms. It becomes significant for leaders to facilitate ethical conduct as their failure to do so hold them as much responsible for behavior as those who benefit from deviant practices.

The ethical orientation of a leader is generally considered to be a key factor in promoting ethical behavior among employees. Leaders need to portray high ethical standards and encourage employees to follow suit, functioning as role models bearing the responsibility to raise the ethical standards of the organization.

The past few decades have witnessed an increasing emphasis on corporate performance, the growing emphasis on quality of life issues, and a spate of recent corporate scandals at such firms as Enron, Tyco, World Com and not forgetting the role of Arthur Andersen. Environmental concerns, rise in the production of hazardous commodities and unfair employment norms have led to the establishment of regulatory agencies like the Environmental Protection Agency, the Equal Opportunity Commission, and the Federal Drug Administration.

CSR and Tobacco Companies

Myth or reality? Major tobacco companies are trying hard to swim against the tide of anti-tobacco activists. Governments and other NGOs are convinced about the killer effects of tobacco and are aggressively campaigning for a tobacco free environment. Companies are trying to face this aggression in many ways are corporate social responsibility is one of the ways adopted. Corporate social responsibility (CSR) can be defined as how businesses align their values. It is about what a company gives back to the society. Considering the negative effects of smoking, tobacco companies are the most vulnerable to attacks from the social activists. There is an increasing hostility between people for and against tobacco production and sales. The lobbies that are favouring tobacco companies include the tobacco farmers, the national tobacco associations, and the multinational tobacco companies; and opposing these are the health workers, the NGO's (consumer groups, media), the academia, and the multilateral organizations like WHO, UNICEF and World Bank.

Issues involved

Most tobacco companies attract constant attention for their line of business. Tobacco is a health hazard. It is also one of the cheapest and most easily available forms of addiction. The sheer magnitude of diseases attached to tobacco addiction is shocking. Most of them are lethal, like cancer and tuberculosis. Over the years, the tobacco companies have been the target of health activists, social workers and other media persons. They are accused of selling life taking substances. For the companies established in this business, it is a catch 22 situation. They also score high on the grounds of employment provided by their operations to millions of people. For the government, tobacco and related products rank among the highest revenue earners.

Advertising is another issue where most tobacco companies are under constant supervision. With a surge in regulations banning direct advertising in any form, the attempt is to move towards surrogate advertising and sponsorships. As an increasing number of countries are banning various forms of direct advertising of tobacco products, tobacco companies have been shifting their attention to indirect promotion of their products by such means as sponsorship of social causes, sports and arts events. For a relatively minor donation to culture, tobacco companies buy their way into the advertising market, where they spend millions of dollars ensuring that the public remains familiar with the colors, logos and images of their brands. ITC sponsoring music conferences and cricket under its Wills brand is a good example.

Major initiatives

Most tobacco companies are heavily into sponsorship of cultural, social and sports events. Social causes like education, medical grants and help to victims of sexual, drug abuse generally top their list. What remains a common initiative among all the tobacco companies is an effort to prevent youth from smoking. Nationwide surveys of stores selling cigarettes over the counter have shown that three out of four sell them to children as young as 11. Between 60-90 per cent of children buy their own cigarettes. In the US, vending machines dispense cigarettes to an estimated 450,000 children every day. More than a million annually become regular smokers, tobacco chewers or cigar chompers. In the US, tobacco sales to minors are illegal in 44 states. The laws, however, are weak and poorly enforced. In this regard, most of tobacco majors try and do what they can to prevent retail access of tobacco to children.

Some even have punitive charges for retailers who violate this law. Companies like R.J. Reynolds, Philip Morris, etc., have been practicing social responsibility since their inception. R.J. Reynolds' history of corporate responsibility began with the company's founder, Richard Joshua Reynolds. He donated generously to the community where he built his business. His first documented gift was in 1891, when he gave US$500 (in today's dollars that would be around US$10,000) toward the establishment of the Slater Industrial School. Slater Industrial is now known as Winston-Salem University.

Most tobacco companies are heavily into sponsoring of cultural, social and sports events.

The British-American Tobacco Ltd. (BAT) does not employ children in their operations. In 2001, it helped establish the Eliminating Child Labor in Tobacco Growing Foundation, following an awareness-raising campaign, which it had begun a year previously, together with the International Tobacco Growers' Association (ITGA) and the trade unions in their sector, the IUF (International Union of Food, Agricultural, Hotel, Restaurant, Catering, Tobacco and Allied Workers' Associations).

For Philip Morris, Corporate social responsibility begins with their products. They believe in telling people about the dangers of smoking doing their best in keeping children away from this product, and at the same time developing potentially less harmful products. But their responsibility doesn't end there. Philip Morris in convinced that a company thrives only when the community around it thrives.

So they generally work with the community and address issues that are of utmost concern. In 2004 they made charitable contributions in 70 different countries, totaling more than US$ 13.6 million.

During the 1890s and early 1900s, Reynolds continued giving private donations to such causes as hospitals, orphanages, new churches, agricultural contests and higher education. Today, R.J. Reynolds employees are given the chance to help direct funds to nonprofit organizations through plans sponsored by the R.J. Reynolds Foundation. Philip Morris set up the Casa di accoglienza delle Donne maltrattate or CADM, in 1986. It is one of Italy's oldest and most active anti-domestic violence organizations. Staffed by a team of volunteers and professionals, it offers refuge, counseling, legal support and practical help to victims of domestic violence. Philip Morris Italy has supported CADM since 2001.

Integrity-Based vs Compliance-Based Approaches to Organizational Ethics

It is important to understand the essential links between organizational integrity and the personal integrity of an organization's members. There cannot be higher-integrity organizations without high- integrity individuals. At the same time, individual integrity is rarely self-sustaining. Even good people can lose their bearings when faced with pressures, temptations and heightened performance expectations in the absence of organizational support systems and ethical boundaries. Organizational integrity, on the other hand, exceeds individual integrity. An important responsibility of leadership in building organizational integrity is to create this ethical framework and develop capabilities to make it operational.

Business Ethics

Ethics is defined as the discipline dealing with what is good and bad, and right and wrong, or with moral duty and obligation. Business ethics encompasses the morality of issues in business. The purpose of business ethics is not to teach the difference between right and wrong but to give people the tools for dealing with moral complexity. Moral values are instilled into each human being at an early age through formal and informal socialization. Although strategic managers adhere to such moral principles in their private lives, some fail to apply them in their professional lives.

Business ethics is important and worthy of serious attention. The behavior of strategic leaders and their awareness of the behavior of employees at all level throughout the organization influence this aspect of corporate culture. These strategic leaders determine the business ethics practiced in an organization.

Sometimes individual mangers or employees adopt certain practices that senior managers regard as unethical. These need to be identified and stopped. If they remain unchecked, they are likely to continue, with the argument that 'everyone does it'. Issues such as insider dealing, salary increments for chief executives, etc. often come to the notice of the public through the media; such issues affect people's perceptions of business in general and at the level of the individual firm. The response of different members of the public varies disproportionately in the sense that some people feel disgruntled and do nothing while others take more strong action through protests and boycotts.

Potential ethical issues must be considered when making strategic decisions. Objectives and strategies should be realistic and achievable rather than over-ambitious and impossible. If the objectives are over-ambitious, the employees may behave unethically.

Organizational values

Organizational values are the enduring beliefs that have worth, merit, and importance for the organization. The crisis in corporate ethics and the crash of once promising companies such as WorldCom, Enron, and Arthur Andersen have brought values to the forefront. One review of recent company failures revealed that unhealthy cultural values played a crucial role in many of the mistakes these companies made.

In considering what values are important for the organization, leaders consider the external environment and the company's vision and strategy. Cultures can vary widely across organizations. However, organizations within the same industry often reveal similar values because they are operating in similar environments. Key values should embody what the organization needs to be effective. Rather than looking at values as either 'good' or 'bad', leaders look for the right combination. The correct relationship among cultural values, organizational strategy, and the external environment can enhance organizational performance.

Building Success through People, purpose and Performance

The success of an organization is governed by the level of bonding it has with its customers; the techniques it employs to please them, give them value-added services and improve customer satisfaction. In addition, the organization should also stay focused on its strategic business plan and objectives for the future. In other words, it should stay connected to its people, customers as well as its corporate goals and ideas.

- Firstly, to connect, there must be an emotional link. Connecting implies building emotion.
- Secondly, to connect, we must create a strong feeling. Most of us do not feel especially connected with our casual acquaintances because we do not feel strongly about them.
- The third part of the definition of connect is to create a positive, uplifting relationship.

Unfortunately in business, people create strong emotional links but the relationship is neither positive nor uplifting. Success is built on the connections we make with people and ideas. Whether it is connecting with customers to improve their service experience, or connecting with the strategic business plan and objectives for coming year, the foundation of success lies in connecting.

Great organizations foster the right kinds of connections between the company, its mission and its employees.

FUNCTIONAL AND OPERATIONAL PLANS IN STRATEGY IMPLEMENTATION

Cost reduction and maintenance of quality can be brought about by effective operational strategies. The first and foremost factor to be taken into consideration is the choice of a good location for the firm's manufacturing facilities.

Location of Manufacturing Facility

In order to achieve the twin objectives of cost minimization and quality maintenance, a company should choose the most efficient locations for its manufacturing facilities. The location of a manufacturing facility depends on the country, the technology and the product.

Country

The host country, i.e., the country receiving the investment, should be economically and politically stable. The company is vulnerable to exchange rate risk when raw materials are sourced from many countries, for manufacturing activity in one or a few countries, and subsequent export to many markets. The parent company might lose its cost competitiveness if the factory is located in the country with volatile exchange rates. Political stability is another important factor in decision making. Change in government may entail changes in investment policies. The FDI policy of a country deals with the extent to which foreign individuals and companies can participate in domestic production activity. The policy also covers local content and sale requirements. The prevalent exit policy and the jurisdiction of courts are other important features of a country's FDI policy. Frequent changes in any of these will affect the functioning of an MNC. Political factors include the lobbying power of domestic industrialists.

Another factor affecting the location of the factory is the level of infrastructural development of the country. Continuous supply of power, sound telecommunication systems, well developed roads and transport facilities make for a favorable destination. Free trade zones (FTZs), export processing zones (EPZs), software technology parks (STPs) and special economic zones (SEZs), which provides tax or other incentives, are facilities created by governments to attract exporters and FDI.

Another important factor in the location decision is the factor costs and productivity in various countries. The factors of production are land, labor, capital and enterprise. The payments for these take the form of rent, wages, interest and profits. MNCs expect to earn some specified return on investment (ROI). Capital and enterprise have become perfectly mobile with the growth in technology and developments in financial markets. So land and labor remain the crucial factors in deciding the location of factories. The literacy rate in the country, the proportion of women and children in the literate population, industrial laws regulating payment of wages, working conditions and employee health and safety laws are other important factors.

Technology

By technology we mean manufacturing technology. The cost of the technology can be important in determining the location of a manufacturing facility. The higher the investment required, the stronger the case for manufacturing in a single or a few locations. If the fixed costs of setting up a manufacturing facility are low, then companies can have locations closer to the market and thereby respond faster to the market demands.

Apart from fixed costs, economies of scale can also help in deciding plant locations. Economies of scale can be defined as the reduction in the per-unit cost of production as a result of an increased scale of operation. Thus, the unit cost of production decreases with increase in production.

Customization and Cost Efficiency

Standardization of products and mass production were till recently considered undeniably cost effective. However, this idea has led to many difficulties particularly in industries like automobiles where the manufacturing process is long. The most serious problem relating to standardization is the inability to change designs in responses to market requirements. Taiichi ohno, the engineer at Toyota developed and implemented lean manufacturing systems in Toyota. The new system removed many of the drawbacks of the conventional manufacturing system and reduced the time required to change dyes on stamping equipment from one day to three minutes.

Product

There are two features of product that determine the location of the manufacturing plant.

1. **Value-to-weight ratio:** Weight of the product has an impact on the transportation costs. Thus, transportation costs for goods of heavy industries are high and justify the location of plants closer to the market. On the contrary, electronic goods have high value-to- weight ratio, i.e., they are expensive but less costly to transport since they are not heavy. In order to achieve economies of scale, electronic goods can be produced at centralized locations. Products such as cement are usually manufactured at locations close to the market since they involve huge transportation costs.
2. **Nature of need-universal or local:** Personal computers and certain industrial products can be

manufactured at centralized facilities, for sale in several markets. On the other hand, consumers often have different tastes and preferences relating to food and personal care products. For these products, manufacturing facilities are usually located nearer to the market.

Product development

Product development involves both new product development and improvement in existing products and manufacturing processes. R&D and product development are futile if they do not generate revenues. One notable exception was IBM, which till the early 1990s focused on long-term research and not on short-term innovation, and assessed the performance of its scientists by their publications and academic honors.

Global Sourcing

An effective way of curtailing financial and operational risks, as well as labor investment inclusive of the plant and the machinery, is done by sourcing components from other manufactures. For example, Sundaram Clayton in India specializes manufacturing radiator caps. It has been awarded the Deming Prize for quality in this item. Rather than investing in the production of this item, automobile manufacturers worldwide prefer to source radiator caps from Sundaram Clayton since it makes them most efficiently. But the primary disadvantage is an increasing reliance on the supplier and the threat of delays in production due to delay to the suppliers. The risk of such dependence has led companies to integrate business activities. The three types of integration are backward, forward and horizontal integration.

To generate economics of scale and reduce the risk of dependence on suppliers, for example, Ford established plants that specialize in the single component, say, air conditioners and supplies them to other locations for the final assembling of cars. Similarly, Airbus Industries, the aircraft manufacturer sources components from numerous locations across Europe and performs the final assembling of aircraft in France and Germany. An alternative to investment in in-house manufacturing of components is for the company to hold equity in the suppliers' firms, giving the company effective control over the cost, reliability and quality of supplies.

Logistics Management in MNCs

Logistics managements enhance reliability and ensure a quick delivery to the manufacturing plant in accordance with the requirements. It essentially deals with the efficient transport of goods. Various impediments like varying time zones, different means of transport, difference in the infrastructure and different laws affect the transport of goods. The means of transport is primarily affected by time and cost concerns. Goods of a perishable nature and edible products possessing a high value-to-weight ratio need to be transported through airplanes rather ships, even though it may increase the expenses.

Logistics is strategic, and not operational as it requires planning and is inter-functional, since the decision affects the firms due to the savings in cost. The quantity, nature of the materials and components, packaging, storage and the distribution chain can all affect the design of the product.

Global Supply Chain Management (GSCM)

Supply chain management is a more comprehensive function than logistics management. It integrates the activities of demand forecasting, procurement, manufacture, distribution and inventory management. MNCs with manufacturing facilities in several countries use logistics information systems (LIS) to reduce delivery time and inventory costs. The challenge of SCM is to mitigate the bull-whip effect. The bull-whip effect is the distortion of actual demand information that occurs as a company moves further away from its customers.

SCM is facilitated by the use of the Internet. Networking tools that connect individual customers and suppliers or provide e-commerce portals have helped improve the information flow between the buyer and supplier thereby strengthening SCM. SCM, in turn, has helped boost the growth of e-commerce transactions. Enterprise resource planning (ERP) helps in connecting suppliers and buyers and helps in managing manufacture, inventory and quality. The widely acclaimed procurement mechanism of Walmart, USA, is an example of the growing partnership between suppliers and buyers.

Transfer of Knowledge from Home Country to Host Country

In the context of MNCs, technology transfer involves sharing knowledge and resources developed by the MNC with subsidiaries or with partners in the host country. Technology includes know-how and machinery. As a result of the implementation of Trade Related Intellectual Property Rights (TRIPS), transfer of Technology has become more expensive since the owners of technology claim more royalty payments. One outcome of TRIPS is that MNCs have started locating manufacturing facilities in developing to benefit from cheap labor. Thus there is no actual transfer of technology, but only a relocation of the production facility. Until recently, the flow of ideas was one-way from the home country to the host country, but now a few MNCs are encouraging research activities in their foreign subsidiaries.

Other issues that can come up are parent-subsidiary relationship. Control over subsidiaries is an important factor in the transfer of technology and affects the relationship between parent and subsidiary. Based on their level of involvement, subsidiaries can be classified into four types-local supplier, international supplier, local developer and product developer.

Unleashing Innovation in Subsidiaries

Innovative ideas do not arise only in headquarters. Therefore, companies should encourage their subsidiaries to innovate. If the parent company focuses on the short-term performance of its subsidiaries, the subsidiaries may avoid new investment avenues and concentrate on protecting wealth. If the parent emphasizes long-term growth and innovation, the subsidiaries may make excessive and unreasonable investment in R&D. Thus, there has to be balance between the two. To ensure that fruitful ideas are encouraged, companies should follow a three-pronged strategy;

- Encourage employees to innovate. Provide incentives for innovation.
- Be a venture capitalist-provide funds to build prototypes and to test-market products.
- Network with subsidiaries and enable interaction.

INTEGRATION OF FUCNTIONAL PLANS

Implementation of strategy involves a wide range of policy decisions to be made including those relating to the functional areas. The purpose of policy as a guide to decision-making is to spell out and clarify strategy, to provide a basis for interpreting strategy which is usually stated in general terms. A carefully selected policy sharpens the meaning of the strategy and guides specific decisions in a direction that supports the strategy. Policy statements have to take into account how all functional plans can be integrated in a cohesive manner.

Thus, policies may be regarded as decisional guides of action that make the strategies work, In a small, single-product firm there is little need for policies to be evolved in the formal sense. A few policies relating to production, purchasing and distribution that are decided to be pursued do not involve consideration of complex issues. In a large organization, however there are many policy issues to be considered in each functional area in the context of multiple decision variables.

The interrelated nature of policies becomes significant as decisional guides are required for managers at different levels in a number of business segments and departments. Establishment of formal policies is therefore, inescapable to provide for consistency in decision-making and predictability of actions. All functional plans need to be seen in totality so that the organization can march faster by deputation of functional plans with clear cut objectives.

Significance of Policies in Reinforcing Functions Plans

The basic purpose of policies as defined above rests on the premise that it is designed to control and reinforces implementation of functional strategies as also major corporate strategies. Control and reinforcement of strategy implementation are facilitated by derived plans in several ways, which also indicate the significance of designing appropriate polices as follows:

1. By limiting discretion and clearly specifying the manner in which things are to be done. Derived plans indirectly control decision-making and actions of functional managers without direct intervention by the top management.
2. By promotion uniformity of handling and similar activities, derived plans facilitate coordination of operations, and thus reduce frictions, which might arise due to discrimination, favoritism, and handling of common functions in different ways.
3. Derived plans, through appropriate policies, lead to consistent patterns of action reflecting the basic aspects of organizational behavior which are institutionalized over time.
4. With standard guides provided, in the policies, decisions can be taken expeditiously without reference to higher level management.

5. By reducing uncertainties in repetitive decisions, derived plans provide a foundation for efficient operation and efforts.
6. In the context of any major change in strategy, policies indicating what actions are contemplated, facilitate acceptance of the policy and thus counteract resistance to the strategic change.
7. Hasty and rash decisions in changing operations can be avoided by managers on the basis of prevailing polices, even when expediency and temporary solutions might require alteration of procedures and practices.
8. Routine matters and ordinary problems are quickly disposed of due to policies offering pre-determined answers to routine problems; thus managers have more time to deal with non-routine and extraordinary problems.

HUMAN RESOURCE STRATEGY

HR policies guide the functioning of HR. These polices provide guidelines for, among other things, recruitment, differentiation among workers in terms of compensation and social responsibility in terms of policies against child labor, etc. HR polices also lay down guidelines for identifying training needs, selecting employees for foreign postings, developing reporting systems and achieving a level of cooperation between the workers' union and management. They also deal with the amount of autonomy that should be given to subsidiaries for devising HR strategies.

It has been argued that MNCs should replicate HR practices in subsidiaries to make the internal environments similar, and to synchronize the performance appraisal and reporting systems of the parent and subsidiaries. Japanese companies, for example, replicate the home country's best practices in the subsidiaries. Some MNCs identify best practices from all their subsidiaries and implement them throughout the organization.

Equality in recruitment and pay

Some companies discriminate against candidates seeking employment on the basis of religion, race, caste, sex or place of birth. Discrimination can take the form of unequal pay, poor working conditions, or restricted access to facilities.

Japan has a male dominated workforce because of discrimination against female candidates. The consequences of differential treatment may range from employee dissatisfaction and industrial unrest to government interference in regulating the organization. Equality in recruitment and pay assumes more importance in the case of MNCs where people from different nationalities are employed.

Types of Staffing Policy

Staffing constitutes the training of individuals for specific functions. Staffing begins with the 'job description'. The nature of the work and the skills required to complete the job have to be identified and described in detail. Staffing also involves selecting people who will fit into the culture of the organization. Companies like GE are more concerned with the applicant's cultural fit than his skills. The staffing policy will also depend on the company's approach to globalization.

Ethnocentric approach

MNCs adopting the ethnocentric approach to globalization view the world as one integrated market place. As a result, they prefer standardization among other things, products, organizational structure and staffing policy. In the ethnocentric approach to staffing, all top management positions are filled by the parent company. Companies exploring emerging markets are often reluctant to recruit locals for senior management positions. They prefer to appoint home country nationals in order to replicate the parent company's corporate culture in the subsidiary.

Polycentric approach

MNCs adopting the polycentric approach to globalization view the world as a differentiated market place requiring customization in every aspect of business. This approach encourages companies to recognize difference in cultures and customize their products, marketing strategy and HR practices accordingly. The major drawback of this approach is the possible lack of coordination between the parent and the subsidiaries due to language barriers and cultural differences. A communication gap between the parent and the subsidiary can also hinder the transfer of technology.

Geocentric approach

In a geocentric approach to globalization, MNCs identify best practices from within and outside the organization and implement them throughout the organization. Applying this principle to staffing, MNCs identify and appoint the most suitable managers regardless of their nationality. The top management also consists of people from a variety of cultures, thus enabling a greater degree of product customization. Training and relocation costs of managers are high in this approach to staffing.

Employing Expatriates

The purpose of expatriation should be clear. Expatriate managers are not mediocre employees in the organization who are sent for training or for a refresher course abroad. They are highly motivated managers who can create and share knowledge. Expatriate managers are residents of the country working in another country for the organization's subsidiary as it is not uncommon for MNCs to depute their employees on contract to other organizations. Companies are empowering their employees with functional responsibilities as against the traditional responsibilities. A global product manager is expected to coordinate all the activities concerning a product in all the countries in which the company operates. This has led to two changes in expatriation. First, the duration of stay abroad for an executive has been reduced. Second, younger employees are also required to work abroad for a few years. Shorter assignments for executives have two benefits: it brings down the costs of expatriation substantially, and it enables working spouses to retain their jobs. Thus, shorter assignments are a win-win situation for both the MNC and the employee.

Developing local talent

MNCs cannot depend entirely on expatriates for running international markets and practices. So, a talented pool of local employees is necessary. Formal training can be given to new recruits through Management Development Programmes (MDPs) conducted by business schools. Alternatively, in-house managers can train new recruits since they are familiar with the processes and culture of the company. The challenge is as much in recruiting and training talented employees as in retaining them.

Training and Development

Training means equipping an individual with the technical or non-technical knowledge for the same specific assignment. Development is a wider term, involving the all-round development of an individual and not necessarily related to a specific job assignment. In MNCs, employee development is necessary to prepare employees to take up future international assignments.

Arranging workshops and MDPs is common in MNCs. MDPs aim at improving coordination among employees with diverse cultural, religious and educational backgrounds. During the course of and MDP, employees develop informal networks and share knowledge.

Job rotation also enables sharing of knowledge. MNCs, therefore, transfer employees to their subsidiaries and give them different functional assignments.

Training of expatriates

Several MNCs offer training to employees to be sent abroad, aimed specifically at overcoming cultural and language barriers that could hinder performance. Some even interview and train the spouses of employees since often it is the spouse who finds it difficult to adjust to cultural changes. An employee has to be trained to adapt to differences in culture, language and lifestyle. Training of expatriates can be broadly classified into three types:

Cultural, language and practical training.

Repatriation of expatriates

Expatriates need to be placed in appropriate positions on their return to the company. Quite often they fail to adjust in their respective giving rise to conflict and resentment. The international experiences of former expatriates can be quite helpful for future expatriates.

Compensation

Compensation includes cash payments and non-cash benefits and perquisites. National differences in pay and the salary of expatriates are key issues in managing compensation. A company's ability to attract talent is linked to its compensation policies. In case of companies with ethnocentric approach, compensation poses no problems as employees belonging to the home country are depute on foreign assignments, i.e., the compensation remains the same as at home.

Companies with polycentric approach develop country-specific plans. Significant problems regarding compensation arise in companies that follow a geocentric approach. In a geo centric approach, the company attempts to create a cadre of 'international managers' who hail from different countries.

Performance Appraisal in Subsidiaries

Performance management incorporates the assessment of performance appraisals with the training of employees, which has a major impact on employees work satisfaction. Employee's regards performance management as fair if the process of evaluation is clearly understood by employees. Research has shown that fair performance evaluation has a positive impact on the job satisfaction of employees. Employees, who were told whether their performance was good or bad soon after completing task, were found to be more satisfied with their jobs than those who received feedback much later. An important aspect of PM is to identify the training and development needs of employees. Research has shown that employees prefer PM that helps them advance their careers to PM which concentrates on past performance.

Domestic HR Strategies pursued in Subsidiaries

International HRM (IHRM) constitutes three approaches, namely, extortive adoptive and integrative. In the extortive approach, the HR pattern prevalent in the home country is exported to the company subsidiaries as well to achieve a general standardization. The integrative approach involves the incorporation of the best practices of all subsidiaries to formulate a uniform strategy across the organization. Quite often managers mix all three strategies. MNCs might follow different approaches for different aspects of HRM. For example, Training may be standardized to ensure quality of teaching in the training programme. Performance appraisal may be undertaken at the local level. The best recruitment process may be identified and implemented across all subsidiaries.

Subsidiaries' Autonomy in Decision Making:

There are three schools of thought operative in the distribution of power between a company and its subsidiaries. These are limited autonomy, variable autonomy, and negotiable autonomy.

Limited autonomy

According to this school of thought, an MNC attitude to globalization affects the relationship between the parent and the subsidiary. Ethnocentric, polycentric or geocentric approaches influence the autonomy of subsidiaries.

Variable autonomy:

Variables like production systems and the country of origin are controllable while uncontrollable constitute political factors, both of which determine the autonomy of a subsidiary. Variable autonomy is also defined as a continuation, along the process of internalization.

Negotiable autonomy

Negotiable autonomy is a constituent of the transnational strategy to globalization, standardizing global practices. The autonomy of a subsidiary is not based on the company; rather it is determined by practices prevalent in the industry. Thus the autonomy of the local manager is decided not by the parent company, but essentially by the best practice, wherever it is being followed. For example, a US MNC having subsidiaries in India and Germany may replicate the recruitment practices of its Japanese subsidiary. Since the Japanese subsidiary has developed the recruitment process that is being implemented at headquarters and in the German subsidiary, it has more negotiable power at headquarters.

Labor Relations

Labor relations refer to the relationship between organized labor and the management. Organized labor refers to trade unions. Labor relations management seeks to maintain a cordial relationship between labor and management, establish a speedy redressal system to minimize losses due to strikes, lock-outs or industrial violence, and promote the participation of workers in management.

Concerns of organized labor

The Indian Industrial Disputes Act, 1947, defines an industrial dispute as 'a dispute' between the employer and worker and other workers, regarding employment, non-employment, terms of employment or conditions of work. Collective bargaining is a tool which employees use to demand more pay, and better working conditions and benefits. Lock-out is a tool which the employer uses to counter there threat of strikes. Since MNCs have the option of relocating their facilities, workers feel insecure about their jobs. They feel that MNCs provide only low-skilled jobs that can be performed as efficiently elsewhere. Workers feel that MNCs could make use of their better bargaining power to impose unfavorable terms on workers.

The strategy of organized labor

Organized labor has tried in vain to counter the bargaining power of MNCs. Labor organizations have attempted to cooperate with each other in countering the bargaining power of MNCs. There are certain fundamental differences in the approaches of trade unions in different countries. Japanese unions do no encourage strikes. In contrast unions in France & Italy wield the weapon of industrial strikes as a legitimate way for workers to settle disputes with management and move wage negotiations in their favor.

Though the international Labor Organization (ILO) and the organization for Economic Cooperation and Development (OECD) have formed guidelines for managements in regards to labor relations, the enforcement mechanisms are not strong enough.

SUMMARY

- This vision of a company's long-term goals and objectives is referred to as the strategic intent.
- Organizations generally describe their goals and intentions in a broad category. This description depicts the company's aims as well as future prospects, providing a vantage point for an organization's future direction and course of business activity.

- The profile of a company depicts the quantity and quality of the company's financial, human and physical resources.
- Strategic analysis enables a firm to identify a range of possible attractive investment opportunities.
- Objectives refer to the purpose behind an action or activity. Annual objectives are the objectives that a firm aims to achieve in one year.
- In order to make the strategic choice, you have to first understand the corporate level factors as well as the business unit-level factors that form the foundation of the strategic choices for the future.
- Leaders play a significant role in developing and sustaining as well as changing, when necessary, an organization's culture.
- In today's progressive and ever-changing world it becomes intrinsic for an integrated approach at various levels of an organization.
- Ethics may be defined as a system or right or wrong. Ethics assists individual in deciding when an act is moral or immoral, socially desirable or not.
- The cost of technology can be important in determining the location of a manufacturing facility.
- Implementation of strategy involves a wide range of policy decisions to be made, including those relating to the functional areas.
- Human resource polices provide guidelines for, among other things, recruitment, differentiation among workers in terms of compensation and social responsibility in terms of policies against child labor, etc.

KEY TERMS

- **Strategic intent:** Vision of company's long-term goals and objectives.
- **Company profile:** Depicts the quantity and quality of the company's financial, human and physical resources.

- **Strategic analysis:** Enables firms to identify a range of possible attractive investment opportunities.
- **Objectives:** refer to the purpose behind an action or activity.
- **Leaders:** Play a significant role in developing and sustaining as well as changing, when necessary, an organization's culture.
- **Ethics:** Defined as a system of right or wrong.
- **Strategy implementation:** Involves a wide range of policy decisions to be made.

ANSWERS TO 'CHECK YOUR PROGRESS'

1. The vision of a company's long-term goals and objectives is referred to as the strategic intent.
2. The profile of a company depicts the quantity and quality of the company' financial, human and physical resources.
3. Multi-business organizations can maximize their shareholder value by focusing on the best combination of business.
4. The strategic position of a company is determined by the influences that the changes in the external environment may have.
5. Leaders are change agents whose success is measured by their efficiency in implementing a strategic vision.
6. Organizational culture can be an effective and positive means of organizational controls.
7. One attribute of a successful leader that has become popular in both the literature and management practice in recent years is emotional intelligence.
8. Two of the ongoing processes of learning organizations are:
    - Empowering employees at all levels
    - Accumulating and sharing internal knowledge

9. The kayo Way serves as the core index of its business to pursue the mission, 'to strive for the wholehearted satisfaction and enrichment of the lives of the people globally'.
10. Economies of scale can be defined as the reduction in the per-unit cost of production as a result of an increased scale of operation.
11. The autonomy of subsidiaries is influenced by ethnocentric, polycentric and geocentric approaches.

QUESTIONS AND EXERCIES

Short-Answer Questions

1. What is an external environment?
2. State any two essential elements of the planning and control system
3. What are the three broad sets of leader's capabilities?
4. Define ethics.
5. How can technology be important to a manufacturing facility?
6. What are the three strategies that companies should follow to ensure that good ideas are encouraged?
7. Define the geocentric approach to globalization.

Long-Answer Questions

1. Explain in detail organizational structure.
2. Evaluate the concept of corporate culture.
3. Explain how it is possible to overcome barriers to change
4. Write detailed notes on emotional intelligence, and the role of Strategic Leadership.
5. How can one create an ethical organization? Explain in detail.

6. Explain in detail functional and operational plans in strategy implementation.
7. Write a detailed note on human resource strategy.

FURTHER READING

Johnson,Gerry and Kevan Scholes. 1994. Exploring Corporate Strategy: Text and Cases. New Delhi: Prentice-Hall of India.

Thompson, Arthur A. and A.J.Strickland. 1997. Strategic Management: Concepts and Cases. Illinois: Irwin Professional Publishing.

Dess, Gregory G., G.T. Lumpkin and Alan B.Eisner. 2008. Strategic Management: Text and Cases. New York: McGraw-Hill/Irwin.

Pearce, John A. and Richard B. Robinson. 1999. Strategic Management. New York: McGraw-Hill.

Kazmi, Azhar. 2002. Business Policy and Strategic Management. New Delhi: Tata McGraw-Hill.

Unit 3

BUSINESS AND STRATEGIC PLANNING

INTRODUCTION

This unit discusses strategic planning and its importance to business. Michael Porter introduced generic strategies to achieve and sustain competitive advantage. Porter's generic strategies aim at increasing the profitability of a firm and stress on strategies incorporated in order to outperform competitors. In this unit, we will be looking at competitive advantage and sustainability. We will also be looking at cost leadership and differentiation in detail. Also, we will be looking at environmental analysis and discussing the concept of environment. We will also be discussing environmental scanning techniques-ETOP, QUEST and SWOT- in detail. Then there is an exhaustive analysis of the components of environment.

UNIT OBJECTIVES

After going through this unit, you will be able to:

- Explain competitive advantage and sustainability
- Discuss cost leadership and differentiation
- Explain environmental analysis and the concept of environment
- Learn about environmental scanning techniques
- Understand the components of environment

COMPETITIVE ADVANTAGE AND SUSTAINABILITY

Michael Porter introduced generic strategies to achieve and sustain competitive advantage. Porter's generic strategies aim at increasing the profitability of a firm and emphasize on strategies incorporated in order to outperform competitors. A general cost leadership is derived from the establishment of a cost position in correspondence with the prices offered by competitors. A firm then lowers the overall cost which in turn affects the entire value chain. Differentiation constitutes the unique value of a product or of services created by a firm, in accordance with the consumer demands. A focus strategy involves the size and composition of the intended, target market; it establishes benefits either through differentiation or a cost leadership, aimed at a narrow segment of the target market. Cost leadership and differentiation strategies are aimed at the entire industry but these strategies are usually employed at a narrow target market.

The following chart illustrates these three strategies on two dimensions: competitive advantage and strategic target.

		Competitive Advantage	
		Uniqueness Perceived by the Customer	Low Cost Position
Strategic Target	Industry Wide	Differentiation	Overall Cost Leadership
	Particular Segment only	**Focus**	

Focus

Before moving on to each generic strategy, it is important to note both casual observation and research support. The incorporation of Porter's forms of competitive advantage lead firms to exceed those which did not. There has been a rich history of strategic management research addressing this topic. One study analysed strategic business units and found that businesses combining multiple forms of competitive advantage (differentiation and overall cost leadership) outperformed business that used only a single form. The lowest performers were those that did not identify with even a single type of advantage. They were classified as 'stuck in the middle'.

COST EADERSHIP

The first generic strategy is overall cost leadership. Cost leadership requires a tight set of interrelated tactics that include:

- Aggressive construction of efficient –scale facilities
- Vigorous pursuit of cost reductions from experience
- Tight cost and overhead control
- Avoidance of marginal customer accounts
- Cost minimization in all activities in the activities in the firm's value chain, such as R&D, service, sales force, and advertising

The experience curve is a primary component of cost leadership, which refers to how a business 'learns' how to lower costs as it gains experience with production processes. That is, with experience, unit costs of production decline as output increases in most industries.

A firm achieving parity is similar to its competitors, or 'on par', with respect to differentiated products. A parity between differentiation and cost leadership results in higher profits in comparison to other rivals in the market. Thus, the cost leader earns above-average returns.

To achieve a low-cost advantage it is necessary to establish a cost benefit relative to the competitor, standard services or services aimed at a wide ranging target market can be employed. However, such a strategy may fail if a firm is unable to attain parity on important dimensions of differentiation such as quick responses to customer requests for services or design changes. ING Direct is a financial services company that provides a 'no frills' service but very generous rates on savings accounts and other services. In part, it succeeds by providing parity on differentiation through very good account security, ease and speed for customers in opening accounts, and very thorough in-line and paper accounts statements.

Improving competitive position vis-à-vis the five forces

A low-cost strategy facilitates high profits even in a highly competitive environment. Also, demands for a rise in input cost by the suppliers can be met effectively, as low-costs ensure an easy adaptability. A low-cost position also serves as an impediment to the progress of economies of scale and cost advantages and further a low-cost position safeguards against substitute products presented by competitors.

Potential pitfalls of overall cost leadership strategies

There are many benefits of following a strategy of overall cost leadership. However, there are some pitfalls as well that must be avoided:

- An excessive focus on one or a few value-chain activities: Firms need to pay attention to all activities in the value chain to manage their overall costs. Very often, managers make big cuts in operations expenses, but don't question year-to-year spending on capital projects. Or managers may decide to cut selling and marketing expenses but leave manufacturing expenses untouched. Managers should explore all value-chain activities, including relationships among them, as candidates for cost reductions.
- All rivals share a common input or raw material: Firms that compete on overall low-cost strategies are vulnerable to price increases in the factors of production. Since they are competing on costs, they are less able to pass on price increases, because customers can easily take their business to competitors who have lower prices.
- The strategy is imitated too easily: One of the common pitfalls of a cost-leadership strategy is that a firm's

strategy may consist of value-creating activities that are easy to imitate.

- A lack of parity on differentiation: As noted earlier, firms endeavoring to attain cost leadership advantages need to obtain a level of parity on differentiation.
- A curtailment of cost advantages as the customer awareness relation to pricing raises.

DIFFERENTIATION

Differentiation is the company of establishing a product or service that is distinguished by the industry as unique, exclusive and valued by customers. Differentiation safeguards against rivalry since brand loyalty lowers the customer's sensitivity to price and by rising a firm's standard pricing it also avoids a need for a low-cost position.

There are various forms of differentiation:

- Prestige or brand image
- Technology
- Innovation
- Features
- Customer service
- Dealer network

Firms may differentiate themselves along several different dimensions at once. For example, BMW is known for its high prestige, superior engineering, and high quality automobiles. Another example is Harley-Davidson, which differentiates itself on the basis of its image and dealer services.

Firms achieve and sustain differentiation advantage and attain above-average performance when their price premiums exceed the extra costs incurred in being unique. For example, both BMW and Harley-Davidson must increase consumer costs to offset added marketing expenses. A differentiator has to justify the price premiums higher than the production cost incurred, through the exclusivity and uniqueness of the product range. However, pricing cannot be completely ignored as a certain level of parity to the competitors needs to be maintained by curtailing costs in areas which do not alter differentiation.

Many firms successfully follow a differentiation strategy. For example, some firms have been able to appeal to a very upscale and discriminating segment of the market by offering products with an excellent image and strong brand identification.

Siebel Systems, a leader in software that manages customer relations, is well known for its customer service. All software requires customer feedback and inputs, with a heavy reliance on client polls. Since its inception sales have ascended to $1 billion, which is faster than any software company, including Microsoft. The CEO of the firm is confident that the firm will sustain its growth rate as long as the company shows respect for the customer.

Differentiation: Improving position Vis-à-vis the five forces

High returns can be earned through differentiation as it provides a safeguard against Porter's five competitive forces. As brand loyalty decreases customer sensitivity to price and increases customer- switching costs differentiation barricades possible competition. Differentiation prevents the need for a low-cost position can also be avoided through differentiation as it increases a company's margins. Thus, brand loyalty and a product's unique features lead to successfully impede competition from entering the market. Differentiation further enables a company to manage supplier power, reducing buyer power, as buyers comparably have fewer choices decreasing their price sensitivity. Also, supplier power decreases as there is great esteem in supplying to a firm producing highly differentiated products and services. Differentiation enhances customer loyalty and averts the danger posed by other substitutes in the market.

FOCUS

Focusing on a particular buyer group, segment of the product line, or geographic market, is a focus strategy. The main difference between cost leadership, differentiation and focus strategies is that while the first two are aimed at the total industry, the third is aimed at servicing a particular target market. This strategy assumes that a firm can serve its strategic target market more effectively than its competitors who serve much bigger markets. A firm can thus obtain the advantages of differentiation and low cost or both. A focus strategy selects target markets where the firm is least vulnerable to substitutes or where competitors are the weakest. An example of this is May Bach, a car from Daimler Benz targeted at the elite group who want customization of the product and do not mind its exorbitant cost.

Risk of Focus

A focus strategy is vulnerable to the following risks.

- Increasing cost differential between broad range competitors and the focus from might offset the differentiation achieved through focus and turn the customers towards firms that offer a broad range of products.
- Perceived or actual differences between products and services might disappear.
- Other firms might find submarkets within the target market of the focus firm and out focus the focuser.

ENVIRONMENTAL ANALYSIS

An organization's business environment encompasses both the external and the internal environment. An organization has to understand the external environment in order to operate effectively in the marketplace. It should also be able to adapt itself to changing circumstances in order to survive in business. The external environment of a firm essentially includes the environment in respect of political, economic, social and technological factors.

CONCEPT OF ENVIRONMENT

An organization's business environment encompasses both the external and the internal environment. An organization has to understand the external environment in order to operate effectively in the marketplace. It should also be able to adapt itself to changing circumstances to survive in business. The external environment of a firm essentially includes the environment in respect of political, economic, social technological, environmental and legal factors.

To make sense of the business environment in this uncertain world, several different influences need to be dealt with effectively in order to conform this uncertainty. These influences can be of the following kinds:

i. **Difficulty in making sense of the diversities involved:** It may be possible to determine varied environmental factors, but they may render infertile, owing to a lack of cohesiveness amongst the prominent influences.

ii. **Speed of change:** Many managers feel that the accelerating technological transformation and the ever growing global communication sector signify a faster change in business as well.

iii. **Problem of complexity:** Managers tend to deal with complication by simplifying them, based on significant historical factors.

Layers of the Business Environment

The most general layer of the environment is often referred to as **macro environment.** This consists of broad environmental factors that impact to a greater or lesser extent on almost all organizations. Particular factors influence various organizations in varying degrees. It becomes significant to locate structural drivers. Which might influence certain kind of organization or organizations?

The next factor is industry. Industry pertains to a general category of organizations generating similar products. It is significant to possess knowledge about consumers to comprehend and enhance the manufacturing structure. Next is the organization that is in the picture. Different organizations compete on different bases. The micro environment of a business includes its customers, employees, suppliers, shareholders, media and competitors.

ENVIROMENTAL SCANNING TECHNIQUES

ETOP

ETOP: A Technique for Diagnosis

Assessment of the environmental information and determining the relative significance of threats and opportunities require a systematic evaluation of the information developed in the course of environmental analysis. For this purpose, preparation of a profile of environmental threat and opportunity (ETOP) is considered to be a useful device. As a summarized depiction of the environmental factors and their impact on future conditions the profile is a convenient means by which attention of top management may be drawn to the most critical factors.

Market environmental analysis (ETOP model- environmental threats and opportunities model) is carried out to understand and give quantitative measure to opportunities and threats that are impelling on the operational space of the company.

Example

Environmental Threat and Opportunity Profile for an engineering company.

Environmental Sector	Impact (+) Opportunity / (-) Threat
Socio- economic	(+) Continued emphasis on infrastructural development which includes power supply for industry, transport, and domestic consumption. (-) Severe resource constraints
Technological	(+) high growth envisaged in industrial production and technology up gradation.
Supplier	(-) sources of technology will become scarce due to formation of technology cartels.
Government	(+) liberalization of technology import policy
Competition	(-) customers will become more discerning in their requirement is due to an increasing role of power plant consultants. (-) Public sector will find it increasingly difficult to retain specialists and highly qualified personnel

An outcome of environmental scanning is likely to be identification of available opportunities. Management should thus be concerned with designing strategies so as to avail of the opportunities with optimum results. The process of designing strategies to that effect is a difficult task. It usually means questioning old methods, exploring unfamiliar environmental waters, facing up to an objective evaluation of strengths and weaknesses, forcing important changes on people in the firm and on organizational arrangements, and taking high risks with the firm's capital. Moreover, it has to be done in a world of rapid change, and it has to be done continuously.

QUEST

QUEST is an acronym for Quick Environmental Scanning Technique. It is a tool designed to identify emerging issues and events that indicate potential threats and opportunities to organizations, to analyse the probable impact of these factors on the organization, and to facilitate the development the appropriate organizational strategies.

The QUEST process

The essential elements of the process are including the criteria for establishing information sources, identifying and analyzing critical trends and events, developing alternative scenarios, identifying strategic options, and selecting options to be incorporated into the strategic management process. An organization could institutionalize an ongoing environmental scanning process to systematically provide information for use in the strategic management program.

QUEST for environmental scanning is a four process:

1. Strategists make observations about the major events and trends in their industry.
2. Then, they speculate on a wide range of important issues that might affect the future of their organizations by scanning the environmental broadly and comprehensively.
3. The Environmental scanner prepares a report summarizing the major issues and their implications, and three to five scenarios incorporating the major themes of the discussion.
4. The report and scenarios are reviewed by the group of strategists who identify feasible strategic options to deal with the evolving environmental conditions. The options are ranked and teams are designated to develop strategies.

SWOT (TOWS)

SWOT Analysis

SWOT is an acronym for strengths, weakness, opportunities and threats. Therefore, SWOT analysis, as the name suggests, is a method that analyses the strengths, weaknesses, opportunities and threats of an individual or a firms. It helps in the formulation of suitable strategies.

The process of strategy formulation begins with situation analysis, i.e., the process of discovering a strategic match between the weaknesses that exist within and the opportunities available outside.

It is a systematic study and identification of those aspects and strategies that best suit the individual company's position in a given situation. The strategy should not only improve an organization's business strengths and utilize the available opportunities, but also get rid of its weaknesses and effectively repel threats.

Strengths

Strengths are the resources, skills or other advantages the firm enjoys relative to its competitors. These are responsible for giving the firm a competitive edge in the market. A company may possess some or all of the following strengths:

- Distinct technical superiority/ best technical know-how
- Financial resources
- Skilled manpower
- Goodwill and image in the market for goods and services
- Access to the best distribution network
- Disciplined and well-mannered employees with high morale and positive attitude
- Top position in the market
- Good customer service/relations

Weaknesses

A weakness is a drawback that acts as an impediment of success or growth. This drawback could be in terms of deficient skills, lack of resources and death of capability. Weaknesses prevent the firm from gaining competitive advantage. Weakness could result from any or all of the following:

- Lack of facilities

- Death of funds or finances
- Poor brand image
- Absence of good managers
- Ineffective management
- Poor marketing skills

Corporate strength and weakness are a matter of interpretation. Understanding the key strengths and weakness of a firm helps to make the search for solutions and alternative strategies narrow. The study of internal strengths and weaknesses provides a useful framework for making the best strategic choice.

Opportunities

Any situation that appears to be in favour of the environment of a firm will be called an opportunity. An environmental opportunity is a situation, which makes it possible for a particular company to enjoy a competitive advantage. For example, changes in the EXIM policy may bring opportunities to some export-oriented companies. Some opportunities for a firm may be:

- Introduction of new technology
- Identification of a new market segment
- Modification in the regulatory environment
- Improvement in seller-customer relationships

Threats

A threat refers to an extremely unfavorable situation in the firm's environment. It is a challenge posed by an unavoidable trend that could lead, in the absence of purposeful action, to the erosion of the company's position. Some threats to a firm may come from:

- A passive market growth
- Entry of resourceful multinational company/ competitors

- Increase in the purchasing power of key customers
- Increase in the bargaining power of main suppliers
- Adverse changes in governmental policies, rules and regulations

Opportunities and threats comprise external influences in the business environment, which change consistently. These opportunities and threats affect organizations to a great extent because organizations operate in a business environment influenced by others. The managers of a firm can identify practical alternatives and realistic options for designing an appropriate strategy provided they understand the opportunities available to the firm and the threats that it may face.

Strengths are the resources, skills or other advantages that a firm enjoys relative to its competitors. Weaknesses, on the other hand, are the deficiencies or limitations of a firm in terms of skills, capabilities and resources. Opportunities present themselves in the form of favorable situation in the firm's environments which make it possible for a firm to enjoy a comparative advantage. Threats refer to the unfavorable situations in the firm's environment or harmful trends that pose a challenge.

Let us take a look at the overview of the global pharmaceutical industry and thereafter arrive at the SWOT analysis of the Indian Pharma market.

Overview of the global pharmaceutical industry

The global pharmaceutical market grew by 7per cent in 2005. North America's pharmaceutical sale grew by 5.2 per cent to $265.7 billion. The region accounts for 47 per cent of global pharmaceutical sales. Europe witnessed comparatively higher growth of 7.1 per cent of $ 169.5 billion. In Latin America the sales grew at an extraordinary 18.5 per cent to $24 billion. Africa and Asia Pacific (excluding Japan) grew by 11 per cent to $46.4 billion. Japan, the second largest pharmaceutical market in the world, had a strong performance in 2005, growing by 6.8per cent to $60.3 billion. The launch of new products, which included thirty molecular entities, in key markets fuelled the 40per cent of the total growth in the Pharma market. It also augurs well for the industry that more than 2,300 products were in clinical development, up 9 per cent from 2004, and up 31 per cent over the past three years. IMS forecast that the total Pharma market, over the next five years, would expand at a compound annual growth rate of 5 to 8 per cent. Europe and North America were projected to grow rate of 5 to 8 per cent pace. Latin America, 7-10 per cent; Asia Pacific/ Africa, 9-12 per cent; and japan at 3-6 per cent.

Indian Pharma Market

The Indian pharmaceutical industry is a successful one providing employment for millions and ensuring that essential drugs at affordable prices are available to the vast population of this subcontinent.

The pharmaceutical industry, which is a subset of the healthcare industry, is the lifeline industry in any economy. Its contribution towards the growth and development of the economy, and towards building a strong human capital and intellectual property rights in a country cannot be undermined.

The setting up the Bengal Chemicals and Pharma Works in 1901 in Kolkata laid the foundation for the Indian pharmaceuticals industry. Till 1970s the industry growth was slow. The total production of formulations and bulk drugs was just Rs.3bn. The Patent Act (1970) and investments by government in the drug industry gave new life to the Pharma sector, catalysing growth from decade to decade. At present there are more than 25,000 manufacturing units in India. Of these more than 15,000 units fall under small-scale sector. From Rs. 3bn in 1970, the overall turnover of the Indian Pharma industry went up to Rs 200bn by 2000. The Pharma industry is now a major foreign exchange earned which has investments both by the private sector as well as the government, and is growing at an annual rate of 9 per cent per annum.

The revenues of the Indian pharmaceutical industry are estimated at $5.5 billion; and according to a survey conducted by the management consultant McKinsey for FICCI, the industry is expected to grow at a phenomenal compounded annual growth of 10 per cent to touch $ 25 billion in revenues by 2010.

The Indian pharmaceutical market is estimate as a $8,790 million market. There is a marked growth in the demand for quality for quality pharmaceuticals and emerging medicines, owing to an increase in lifestyle-related diseases attributed to an increasing population. In March 2005, the Indian Patents Third Amendment Bill established patent protection for pharmaceutical products in India. Bringing forth transformation in the industry, raising India's global prospects.

SWOT Analysis of Indian Pharma Industry

Strengths

- Good accessibility to well-trained scientists.
- Strong distribution and marketing network.
- Rich biodiversity.
- Competencies in process development and chemistry.
- Competitive cost.
- Strong manufacturing base.
- Well-developed industry.

Weaknesses

- Need for developing strong linkages between academia and the industry.
- Low healthcare spend and medical expenditure on national level.
- Tarnishing of industry's image at home and abroad due to production of low-quality and spurious drugs.
- Little investment in pioneering research and development.

- Inability to compete with multinational companies due to lack of resources.
- Not very successful in 'new drug discovery research' and commercialization of molecules on a worldwide basis.
- Opportunities
- Scope for contract manufacturing agreements with MNCs.
- Potential of the country as a centre for international level clinical trials.
- Niche player in global pharmaceutical research and development.
- Generic drugs supply to developed markets.
- Considerable export potential
- Licensing deals for NCEs and NDDS with MNCs.
- Sell products from multinational companies in the domestic market through market alliances.

Threats

- Serious challenge to domestic industry from product patent regime. The industry needs to invest in research and development to counter this.
- Lack of enabling regulatory requirement hampers research and development effort by pharmaceutical companies. Example: Restrictions on animal testing
- Outdated patent office.
- Unrealistic ceilings on product prices with the drug price control from the government. This prevents pharmaceutical companies from generating required profit margins.
- Lowering of tariff protection.
- The existence of many small-scale Pharma units is threatened by the new MRP-based excise duty regime (especially in Andhra Pradesh and Maharashtra, which were involved in contract manufacturing. These companies

are shifting their manufacturing units to states like Jammu and Kashmir that enjoy tax holidays.

COMPONENT OF ENVIRONMENT

External Environment: PESTEL Framework and Scenario Analysis

Strategies are operative in the responsible to the external business environment. The efficiency or productivity of a firm has to be read in the context of its external conditions. Forecasting is a medium of examining various environmental trends. Forecasts comprise environmental monitoring and scanning to identify prevalent trends. It becomes significant to understand the rival's knowledge and information to develop forecasts and scenarios in order to focus on present probabilities and curtail future challenges.

The general external environment will be seen in the context of two frameworks-PESTEL Framework and Scenario Analysis.

PESTEL Framework

The word 'PESTEL' is short for Political, Economic, Social, Technological, Environmental and Legal. Let us now discuss each of the components of the framework in detail.

Political environment

The rules and regulations of a country are deeply influenced by the political forces. All firms operating in a country adhere to these rules and regulations which are formed by government to protect consumers and the local environment. These regulations and political constraints for the firms come in the form of pricing policies, anti-trust laws, tax programmes, legislation of minimum use, pollution policies, fair-trade decisions, administrative activities, etc. These laws, rules and regulations affect a company's profits. However, there are other political actions such as patent laws, government subsidies and product research grants that support business activities. Thus, political forces have a positive as well as negative influence on the organization. Political activity also influences three additional functions- supplier function, customer function and competitor function.

The supplier function is influenced by political activity when any private business is dependent on government-owned resources and national stockpiles of agricultural products. This dependence undoubtedly affects the firm's strategies.

As regards the customer function, government demand for products and services can create, sustain, enhance or eliminate many market opportunities.

Similarly, when the government takes precautions to protect consumers and local industries, its decisions greatly affect businesses. So, the government's actions are of great concern to every firm. Firms analyse the government's strategies and develop complementary plans that can help them in exploiting the opportunities

Economic environment

Economic environment, as the name suggest, is concerned with the economic condition of the consumers and the market. Before formulating strategic plans, it is important of study the macroeconomic trends in the market which cover the following:

i. Trends in the growth of the gross national products or GNP

ii. Inflation rates

iii. Disposable income

iv. Propensity to spend (nationally and internationally)

v. Prime interest rates

Each and very market is unique because the pattern of consumption in each of them is different. The consumption pattern in the different market segments depends on the wealth of the consumers that keeps fluctuating and affects their buying behavior.

Social environment

The social environment is a very important factor as changes in the values, beliefs, attitudes, opinions and lifestyles in society create potential opportunities for an organization. In order to grow, a company should take advantage of societal changes. The cultural, demographic, religious, educational and ethnic conditioning of individuals in society affects the social environment.

Since the middle of the twentieth century, a large number of women have started working outside their homes. Women in the workforce have decisively affected the hiring and compensation policies and resource capabilities of firms that employ them. They have also created a demand for a wide range of products and services necessitated by their absence from home. A whole range of products and services such as convenience foods, microwave ovens and day-care centres, have entered the market on account of this social development.

Technological environment

All factors related to the materials and machines used in manufacturing goods and services are categorized as technology.

A very important consideration in a technology-intensive business is the expenditure on technology. Similarly, the rate of change of technology influences the decisions in various organizations. The receptivity to new technology and its adoption by the public also has an impact on decisions made in an organization. Technological innovations determine how organizations compete and thrive in the marketplace.

Environmental forecasting

As mentioned earlier, the tools used for environmental forecasting are as follows:

i. Environmental scanning

ii. Monitoring

iii. Competitive intelligence

For managers to be able to make accurate forecasts, these tools should be capable of giving results that are reliable. Otherwise, the raw material provided by environmental scanning, monitoring, etc., will be rendered useless in forecasting. As the word 'forecasting' suggests, the purpose of environmental forecasting is to predict the changes that are likely to take place in the environment, the speed with which they will take place, their intensity, their direction as well as their scope. It will also study the time that will be required for any new technology to enter the market, the formation of new legislations in the context of an issue raised, the trends and lifestyles that exist and whether they will continue or die out.

Scenario analysis/planning

Scenario analysis involves more detailed and deep forecasting. This analysis covers subjects like demographics, economics and psychology. It analyses the trends prevalent in society, the technology available and likely to be developed, the political scene, the condition of the economy, etc., because all these may affect the issue being discussed. Take Lego, for example, the famous Danish toy manufacturing company. It holds one of the topmost positions in the construction segment of the toys market. However, if some drastic change occurs in the toys market, the company may find its market shrinking steadily. This is because Lego is not the only player in this market. Competition gets tougher with more and more children spending time at the computer. Lego obviously has many competitors, including computer-based game and toy manufacturers. Some of its competitors are even technologically more superior. Besides, there will be many more inventions ready to enter the market and pose fresh threats.

To keep such losses and adverse effects at bay, efficient managers will always look at the future in a wider context, that is, far beyond the existing, conventional or set guidelines in anticipation of the changes that might take place ten years down the line. Let us take the example of Shell Oil Company which effectively used various tools of analysis along with other information collected to create scenarios regarding possibilities or possible results or repercussions in the1960s and 1970s. Its strategic planning, with effective use of scenarios, had prepared the company well in advance for the steep rise in the prices of crude oil, the scarcity of gasoline and a general depression in the global economy that resulted from the oil embargo in 1973. As a result, the company was able to foresee the instability in the environment and the focus of power shifting to the oil producers. With enough time to think over the repercussions and consider various options, the company was able to identify the risk factors involved and explore corrective options or solutions.

The company's process of scenario planning was done in six stages:

i. People from within the organization were interviewed and asked for their honest opinions. People external to the business were also asked open-ended questions that demanded frank answers.

ii. The responses received in the interviews were analysed according to the issues. This naturally led to the creation of a processing agenda.

iii. Each agenda was synthesized in order to bring out the uncertain or disputable issues and their relationship with each other.

iv. Workshops were organized to identify plausible repercussions and create scenarios that may come into existence ten to fifteen years down the line.

vi. The strategy options were tested keeping in mind the scenarios to judge their effectiveness.

Legal

While scouting for opportunities in the environment, corporate try to seek out investment destinations where legal framework is quite stringent. By legal framework it could mean monopolies legislation, employment law, health and safety, product safety, human rights issues, etc. Generally firms try to locate in such areas where legal matters are simplified and transparent ways of dispute resolutions exist.

SUMMARY

- Cost leadership requires a tight set of interrelated tactics.
- A low-cost strategy facilitates high profits even in a highly competitive environment.
- Differentiation is the concept of establishing a product or service that is distinguished by the industry as unique, exclusive and valued by customers.
- Focusing on a particular buyer group, segment of the product line or geographic market, is a focus strategy.
- An organization's business environment encompasses both the external and the internal environment.
- The most general layer of the environment is often referred to as the macro environment.
- There are three major types of environmental scanning techniques- QUEST, ETOP and SWOT.
- Strategies are operative in a responsible to the external business environment. The efficiency or productivity of a firm has to be read in the context of its external condition.

KEY TERMS

- **Cost leadership:** the first generic strategy in strategic planning.
- **Differentiation:** Concept of establishing a product or service that is distinguished by the industry as unique, exclusive and valued by customers.

- **Focus strategy:** Focusing on a particular buyer group, segment of the product line, or geographic market.
- **QUEST:** Acronym for Quick Environmental Scanning Technique.
- **SWOT:** Acronym for strengths, weakness, opportunities and threats.
- **PESTEL framework:** Short for Political, Economic, Social, Technological, Environmental and Legal.

ANSWERS TO 'CHECK YOUR PROGRESS'

1. Two interrelated tactics of cost leadership are:
    - Aggressive constructions of efficient-scale facilities
    - Tight control and overhead control
2. The various forms of differentiation are:
    - Prestige or brand image
    - Technology
    - Innovation
    - Features
    - Customer service
    - Dealer network
3. One risk that focus strategy is vulnerable to is:
    - Perceived or actual differences between products and services might disappear.
4. Industry impacts organizations. Industry pertains to a general category of organization generating similar products.
5. All factors related to the materials and machines used manufacturing goods and services are categorized as technology and form the technological environment.

QUESTIONS AND EXERCISES

Short- Answer Questions

1. What is cost leadership?
2. List any two pitfalls of overall cost leadership.
3. Write short notes on the three types of influences required to better understand the business environment.
4. What is PESTEL Framework?

Long-Answer Questions

1. Explain differentiation in detail
2. What is focus strategy? Elaborate.
3. Write a detailed note on the concept of environment.
4. Describe ETOP and QUEST.
5. What are components of environment? Analyze in detail.

FURTHER READING

Johnson, Gerry and Kevan Scholes. 1994. Exploring Corporate Strategy: Text and Cases. New Delhi: Prentice-Hall of India.

Thompson, Arthur A. and A.J.Strickland. 1997. Strategic Management: Concepts and Cases. Illinois: Irwin Professional Publishing.

Dess, Gregory G., G.T. Lumpkin and Alan B.Eisner. 2008. Strategic Management: Text and Cases. New York: McGraw-Hill/Irwin.

Pearce, John A. and Richard B. Robinson. 1999. Strategic Management. New York: McGraw-Hill.

Kazmi, Azhar. 2002. Business Policy and Strategic Management. New Delhi: Tata McGraw-Hill.

Unit 4

CORPORATE LEVEL STRATEGIES

INTRODUCTION

Decisions made at the corporate level of organizations are those which significantly affect business units. In this Unit, we shall be discussing the various strategies used at the corporate level. We will be discussing the concept and importance of core competence. Corporate level and industry level analysis has also been discussed in detail. Then there are exhaustive explanations on quality factors in strategic choice and factors affecting strategic choice. The four key questions of corporate strategy have also been briefly covered. There is also a detailed explanation of strategic analysis and Ansoff's product market matrix.

UNIT OBJECTIVES

After going through this unit, you will be able to:

- Explain corporate-level strategies and tactics
- Discuss corporate-level and industry-level analysis
- Discuss qualitative factors in strategic choice
- Learn about profit impact on market strategies and Ansoff's product market matrix

CORPORATE LEVEL STRATEGIES

Strategic decisions made at the corporate level of organizations are those which significantly affect business units. Managers at this level act on behalf of shareholders and other stakeholders to provide services and, quite possibly, strategic guidance to business units. These business units themselves seek to generate value by interacting with customers. In such circumstances, a key question is: 'to what extent and how the corporate level might add value to what the business does; or at least how it might avoid destroying value?'

The four key questions which form the basis for corporate level strategies are:

- What is the overall rationale of the corporate parent in terms of how it envisages itself enhancing the value created by the business units for its shareholders/ stakeholders?
- What is the logic of the mix of business units in the corporate portfolio? How does this make sense in terms of the corporate rationale?
- Is the extent and type of diversity of the corporation sensible, given the corporate rationale and logic of the portfolio? The focus is on the nature and extent of diversification.
- How do corporate parents and business units interact? Is the nature of corporate control of subsidiaries appropriate in terms of the previous issues discussed, namely the corporate rationale, the logic of the portfolio and the extent of diversity?

Stability, Expansion, Retrenchment and Combination Strategies

Mergers and acquisitions

Mergers can be defined as the integration of two or more firms on a co-equal basis. In mergers, the concerned firms pool all their resources together to create a sustainable competitive advantage. An acquisition on the other hand, refers to the process of gaining complete or partial control of a company by another company for some strategic reasons. Unlike mergers, acquisitions can sometimes be unfriendly or hostile. This implies that a firm attempts to take over another firm by adopting hostile measures which may not be in the interest of the acquired firm. This trend is spreading rather quickly.

Historical perspective of mergers

1. The pattern that emerged with the first merger wave dating back to 1897 lasted till 1904. It was basically an outcome of the industrial revolution. It led to the establishment of large industrial houses, which are still present in the US and many other corners of the world. Mergers during this period were mainly horizontal.
2. The second merger wave started around the 1920s and lasted till 1929. This period was marked by vertical and conglomerate mergers. This period saw the emergence of sectoral clusters in railroads and utilities.
3. The period between 1965 and 1975 can be termed as the period of the third wave of mergers. During this period the emphasis was more on achieving economies of scale by the mass industrial production of consumer goods.
4. The fourth merger wave happened during the period 1984 to 1988 when more mergers took place in Europe than in the US. In this period, the emphasis was on creating synergies. Technology played an important role during the period.
5. The fifth merger wave which started in 1995 was characterized by words like globalization a deregulation. As a result of globalization, markets expanded and the size of the firms also grew. As a result of deregulation, industries which earlier enjoyed a monopoly were exposed to competition from private and international players.

Going by historical evidence, the increase in merger activity can be seen as a reaction to the changing business environment. These changes may vary from time to time and are mostly related to changes in technology.

Rationale for mergers and acquisitions

The reasons for opting for mergers and acquisitions vary from one firm to the other. We will now look at some of the common reasons:

Increased market power

The primary reason for firms going in for mergers and acquisitions is their desire to increase their market power. A firm gains market power, when it is able to sell its goods or services at a price which is lower than its competitors or is lower than the cost of producing the product or service. A firm may have core competencies but may lack the required resources and size to compete in the market. Thus, most mergers and acquisitions which take place with the intention of increasing market power target competitors, suppliers, distributors or business in related industries. In order to expand the size of the firm, firms go for horizontal, vertical and conglomerate mergers.

Horizontal mergers

A merger between two firms operating and competing in the same business activity is known as a horizontal merger. Combining two business entities results in a larger firm and thus greater economies of scale. However, it is not the only reason for the popularity of horizontal mergers. Though horizontal mergers benefit from large scale operations, not all firms merge horizontally to achieve economies of scale. Firms may merge horizontally to share resources and skills and also to derive synergy. Governments make efforts to regulate horizontal mergers as they can minimize competition. By decreasing the number of firms in an industry, a horizontal merger may create a monopoly market causing the consumers to suffer. The proposed merger between GE and Honeywell, for instance, was stopped by European authorities, fearing monopolization in the industry. The merger between Deccan Aviation and Kingfisher Airlines is also a good example for a horizontal merger.

Vertical mergers

When two firms in the same industry but in different stages in the value chain merge, it is called a vertical merger. There are different reasons for companies entering into vertical mergers. Vertical mergers can be entered into due to any of the following reasons:

i. Reduction in the costs of communication

ii. Production coordination

iii. Better planning for inventory and production

Coke and Pepsi, for example, acquired many bottling companies to improve marketing and supplying facilities. Similarly, to maintain greater control on the prices of tea leaves, Hindustan Unilever Limited and Tata Tea purchased many tea gardens in Assam and West Bengal.

Conglomerate mergers

When two firms from unrelated business activities merge, it is known as conglomerate merger. Conglomerate mergers can be categorized into three different types:

i. Product extension merger

ii. Geographic extension merger

iii. Pure conglomerate merger

When two firms in a related business activity merge, it is called a product extension merger. This helps broaden the product line of firms. When two firms operating in non-overlapping geographic areas merge, it is known as geographic extension merger. When two firms from unrelated business activities, it is known as a pure conglomerate merger. Apart from increasing the market power there are many other reasons that have contributed to the increase of merger and acquisition activities.

Overcoming entry barriers

When firms try to enter new markets, they often face many problems, some of which may act as barriers to their entry. Well established firms may sell their products and services in large volumes thereby gaining economies of scale. These economies of scale act as barriers to entry. Another barrier that a new entrant in the market faces is product loyalty. An entrant in a new market prefers differentiating its products from its competitors. Thus, economies of scale, product loyalty and high advertising expenses act as barriers for a firm trying to enter a new market. The greater the barriers to entry, the more the likelihood that firms will take to mergers and acquisitions to overcome the barriers.

1. Cost of new product development

Developing new products and launching them successfully in the market not only requires commitment of the firm's resources but the return on investment may take a long time. Moreover, the market acceptance of the new product is also unpredictable. According to a research, 88 per cent of new products fail to achieve expected results while 60 per cent of innovative products are copied within four years of being patented.

Firms prefer mergers and acquisitions in order to avoid the internal costs of developing new products. Moreover, mergers and acquisitions also reduce the risks associated with the launch of new product, as the product is already tested in the market. If a company acquires another company that already has an established product in the market, the acquiring company can enter the market more quickly.

2. Increased speed to market

As discussed earlier, mergers and acquisitions lead to faster market entry when compared to the time taken for new product development. Research has shown that mergers and acquisitions are the quickest route to new markets and new capabilities. The new capabilities can be used to introduce new products and enter markets, and this can create can advantageous market position. However, how long the advantage may last, depends upon the rivals' competitive responses.

3. Lower risk compared to developing new products

Developing a new product involves a lot of risk. Managers view mergers and acquisitions as a risk-free method of gaining entry into new markets. However, one major drawback associated with increasing mergers and acquisitions is that they prevent investments in new product development. Research shows that mergers and acquisitions have become a means to avoid risky internal ventures. Many firms prefer not to incur heavy expenses in developing new products, as acquisitions often seem to provide an economically more viable option.

4. Increased diversification

A firm finds it easy to develop and introduce new products in a market where it has some experience. On the contrary, if a firm launches a product that has no relation to its existing portfolio of products, there are lower chances of its success. Thus, in order to diversify, firms would prefer the mergers and acquisitions route as it can be used for both related as well as unrelated diversification. Therefore, mergers and acquisitions are more common when firms want to diversify on a global level.

5. Reshaping the firm's competitive scope

The intensity of competition affects the profitability of firm. To reduce the negative effect of competition, and also to reduce their dependence on a single or a few products, firms acquire other firms. If a firm is dependent on a single product for all its revenues and profits, the competitive scope of the company is likely to be reduced. To avoid dependence on a single product, many firms venture into new industries through acquisitions.

Reasons for Cross-Border Mergers and Acquisitions

There are various reasons for the increasing number of cross-border mergers and acquisitions. Some of these reasons are growth, technology, government policy, differential labor costs, productivity and source of raw materials.

1. Growth

Growth is one of the primary motivation factors for cross border mergers and acquisitions as they provide an opportunity for firms to grow fast. A firm making profits in an ailing economy would not like to make additional investments in the same country. It makes perfect business sense for the firm to invest in an economy which promises faster growth. Firms which have operations in one particular country may not have a cost advantage because of limited sales. If the operations are expanded to other countries, due to the economies of scale, the firm can gain cost advantage.

2. Technology

A technology superior firm may go in for mergers and acquisitions to exploit its technological advantage. On the other hand, a firm which lacks technological advantage may go for mergers and acquisitions to gain access to superior technology. By using the advanced technology of the acquired firm, the acquirer can improve its competitive position and profitability both at home and abroad.

3. Government policy

Government policies and regulations relating to tariffs and quotas can have a major impact on mergers and acquisitions. If a country imposes tariffs and quotas to protect its domestic industry, exports will suffer. Environmental and other regulations can increase the time and cost required to build facilities for entry abroad. Thus, acquiring a company with facilities in place makes good business sense.

4. Differential labor costs and productivity

Labor costs comprise a significant portion of the cost of production. Many multinational companies go in for mergers and acquisitions to take advantage of the availability of cheap labor. It is because of this reason that many multinational companies are heading towards developing countries like India and China to set up their manufacturing bases. Higher productivity of labor also influences cross-border mergers and acquisitions.

5. Source of raw materials

The factor plays an important role in the growth of vertical mergers, more so for acquiring firms from resource-poor domestic economies. This approach may not be feasible in the case of strategic raw materials as many countries have restrictions on foreign ownership of such assets.

Corporate Restructuring

Restructuring can be defined as a strategy by which a company changes its business or financial structure. Restructuring also involves making radical changes in the composition of the business. GE witnessed tremendous growth during the tenure of Jack Welch (1981- 2001). Many analysts attribute GE's success to its effective use of restructuring strategies. As a CEO, Jack Welch sold 350 businesses for a total of $23.8 billion and acquired some 900 businesses for a total of $ 105.5 billion. Under Jack Welch, restructuring became a continuous process, resulting in the creation of greater efficiencies and globalization of operations. The success of GE highlights the importance of restructuring in a competitive business environment.

Firms use restructuring strategies in response to the changes in the external and internal environment. In the light of rapid environmental changes, restructuring is one of the best strategies for companies to create maximum value for their stakeholders.

Between the 1960s and the 1990s, diversification became a common phenomenon. Many firms diversified to an unmanageable extent. Over diversification led to an increase in bureaucratic inefficiencies and the performance of these companies was adversely affected. As a result, stock prices of these companies fell drastically, making them soft targets for hostile takeovers. To minimize such risks, firms have to undertake restructuring activities.

Form of restructuring

Restructuring can happen in the form of expansions, sell-offs corporate control and changes in ownership structure.

Expansion can take place through mergers and acquisitions, tends offers or joint ventures. Sell-offs can take place through spin-offs, split-offs, split-ups, divestitures and equity carve-outs.

Corporate control can be achieved by premium buy-backs, standstill agreements, anti-takeover amendments and proxy contests. Changes in ownership structure can be brought about by going private and through exchange offers, share repurchases and leveraged buy-outs.

The various forms of restructuring are discussed in detail in the following pages:

Expansion

Firms can expand their operations through mergers and acquisitions, tender offers and joint ventures. A merger can be defined as any transaction through which two or more firms integrate their operations on a relatively co-equal basis. It is a transaction that forms one economic unit from two or more previous ones. Different firms have different resources and capabilities and bringing them together can lead to the creation of competitive advantage. As already discussed, mergers can be classified as horizontal, vertical or conglomerate mergers. The various types of mergers have already been discussed in detail earlier.

In a tender offer, a company which intends to acquire a controlling interest in another company asks the shareholders of the target company to submit or tender their shares of stocks in the firm. If the company wants to take over control of another company, it has to first take approval from the target company's management and the board of directors of the target company. An alternate approach known as the bear hug can also be adopted. In this approach, a company communications with the directors to the target company regarding its acquiring company does not get the approval; it can directly appeal to the stockholders through tender offers. If the company obtains a favorable response to the tender offer, the acquiring company can gain control over the company and replace the directors who did not cooperate in the takeover effort. This type of taking control is referred to as a hostile takeover.

A target company, in order to avoid being taken over, may join hands with another company with which it would like to form an association. The organization with which the target company wants to form an association is referred to as a White Knight. To avoid another company from taking over, the target company can also go for some form of restructuring such as offering shareholders a large cash dividend financed by debt. Shareholders prefer this form of restructuring to an outside offer, making the target less financially attractive to the bidder. In a joint venture, the participants continue to exist as separate firms with the joint venture representing a newly created entity. Partners share a proportional capital, distinctive skills, personnel, reporting systems and technologies to gain competitive advantage. Joint ventures result in a collaborative approach among the partners to create new value.

2. Sell-offs

There are two major types of sell-offs: spin-offs and divestures. A spin-off results in the creation of a separate legal entity, the shares are distributed among existing shareholders of the parent company on a prorate basis. It is a form of dividend to existing shareholders. The new entity has the power to make independent decisions. It can also develop policies and strategies which are different from those of the parent company.

There are two types of spin-offs: split-offs and split-ups. In a split-off, some of the existing shareholders receive stocks in a subsidiary in exchange of stock of the parent company. In a split-up, the entire firm is fragmented into a series of spin-offs. This is to ensure that the parent firm no longer exists and the new company created as a result to split-up survives in the long run. Unlike spin-offs, where only shares are transferred or exchanged, divestures involve the sales of a portion of the firm to a third party. Since the buyer is an existing firm, no legal entity is created.

Equity carve-outs is a variation of divesture. In this, a portion of the firm is sold to outsiders through an equity offering, giving them ownership of the previously existing firm. Equity carve-out also result in the creation of a new legal entity.

3. Corporate control

Corporate control can be established through premium buy-backs, standstill agreements, anti-takeover amendments and proxy contests. In premium buy-backs, a substantial stakeholder's ownership interest is re-purchased at a premium that is above the market price. In connection with such buy-backs, a standstill agreement is often signed. A standstill agreement is a voluntary contract in which a shareholder whose shares have been purchased agrees that he or she will not make further attempts to take over the company in the future. If a buy-back is not involved in the standstill agreement, the stockholder with substantial influence agrees not to increase his or her ownership control.

Anti-takeover amendments refer to changes made in corporate bylaws to prevent mergers and acquisitions. Some of them are as follows:

i. Super majority voting provisions, which require a very high percentage of stockholders to approve the merger.

ii. Unspecified service terms for directors which can delay change of control for a very long period.

iii. Golden parachutes wherein large termination payments have to be made to the existing management

In proxy contests, a peripheral category often referred to as 'dissidents' or 'insurgents' gains access to the company's board of directors curtailing the control of other members of the board. Proxy contests are mainly aimed at the prevalent management.

4. Changes in ownership structure

This includes exchange offers, share repurchases, going private and leveraged buy-outs. An Exchange offer implies replacing debt or preferred stock or common stock or exchanging common stock for debt or preferred stock. The first type of exchange increases leverage while the second type decreases leverage. The ownership structure can also be changed by repurchasing shares, i.e., a company can buy back some portion of its outstanding shares of common stock. The percentage of shares purchased may vary. If it is successful in purchasing a substantial percentage of shares, it can change the control structure of the company.

A going-private transaction involves a small group of investors purchasing the entire equity interest in a public company. When the members of the incumbent management group initiates the transaction (purchasing substantial proportion of the equity ownership of the new private company), it is known as a management buy-out. A small group of outside investors may provide funds and secure representation on the private company's board of directors. They may also arrange finance from third-party investors. When the private company borrows substantially from third parties, such transactions are called leveraged buy-outs (LBOs).

Restructuring vs reengineering

In the 1990s huge companies like IBM, Philips, Texas Instruments, Sears, Digital Equipment, etc. suffered from falling profits.

The industrial terrain changed faster than the top management could remodel its basic beliefs and assumptions about markets, technologies, customers and employees. As such the difference in the pace of change in an industry and that in an organization necessitates organizational transformation. This transformation could include downsizing, overhead reduction, and employee empowerment, process redesign and portfolio rationalization. In order to avoid this painful process of restructuring, it is important that a firm anticipates and creates its own future

1. Restructuring has high social costs. An individual firm might avoid these, but society cannot avoid the. In these circumstances it leads to plummeting employee morale and employees feel they are the most expendable assets.
2. Restructuring rarely results in fundamental improvement in the business, it only lends time for improvement. In order to avoid the painful process of restructuring, it is important that a firm anticipates and creates its own future.

Qualitative difference between reengineering and restructuring

1. Reengineering offers the hope of becoming better while getting smaller. In contrast, any company that is restructuring seriously will find itself getting smaller much faster, than it is getting better.

2. Restructuring may be considered a necessary evil, whereas reengineering can be positive and beneficial even as it is undertaken. Reengineering for many companies is aimed at catching up with rivals rather than moving out in front and lead.

   When US car companies were matching Japanese companies in terms of cost and quality, Japanese manufacturers were erecting new competitive barriers: breathtaking engine performance, razor-edge handling, luxury, new design aesthetics and product lifestyle aimed at lifestyle niches.

Concept of Synergy

The degree to which two or more activities or processes complement each other to the extent that their combined effect is greater than the sum of the part is called synergy. Synergies can arrive out of the fact that for a diversified firm, two firms may share a common distribution system. Also during the merger of two companies, potential synergies are looked at, which would make the merger successful in terms of sharing or utilizing facilities, products, knowledge, etc.

To accomplish successful related diversification, a company must combine multiple facets of its business to create synergies across the organization. Procter & Gamble (P&G) is a prime example of such a firm. Using related diversification, it creates synergies by leveraging core competencies, sharing activities, pooling negotiating power, and vertically integrating certain form a speech by P&G's CFO, illustrates how the company has used the concept of synergy to its best.

Remarks to financial analysts

'Today we sell 10 brands with sales of one billion dollars or more. Seven of these 10 brands surpass the billion-dollar sales marks during the 1990s. And in total, these 10 brands accounted for more than half of our sales growth during the decade. Beyond these 10, there are other brands with the potential to achieve a billion dollars in sales by 2005.

P&G's unmatched line-up of billion dollar leadership generates consistently strong returns. In virtually every case, P&G's leading brands achieve higher margins and deliver consistently strong shareholder returns. Having a stable of such strong global brands creates significant advantages for P&G- and our total company scale multiplies those advantages.

We can obviously take advantage of our purchasing power for things as varied as raw materials and advertising media. We can leverage the scale of our manufacturing and logistics operations. But we can do far more.

We have the scale of our intellectual property-the knowledge and deep insight that exists throughout our organization. We have scale in our technologies – the enormous breadth of expertise we have across our product categories. There is scale in our go-to-market capabilities and our global customer relationships.'

CORPORATE LEVEL TACTICS

The choice of location and site follows an assessment of demand, size, and input requirements. Location refers to a fairly broad area like a city, an industrial zone, or a coastal area. The choice of location is influenced by a variety of considerations: proximity to raw materials and markets, availability of infrastructure, governmental policies, and other factors.

Proximity to Raw Materials and Markets

An important consideration for location is the proximity to sources of raw materials and nearness to the market for final products. In terms of a basic locational model, the optimal location is one where the total cost (raw material as transportation cost plus production cost plus distribution cost for the final product) is minimized. This generally implies that:

i. A resource-based project like a cement plant or a steel mill should be located close to the source of basic material.

ii. A project base on imported material may be located near a port.

iii. A project manufacturing a perishable product should be as close to the centre of consumption.

Availability of Infrastructure

Availability of power, transportation, water and communications should be carefully assessed before a location decision is made.

Government Policies

Government policies have a bearing on location. In the case of public sector projects, location is directly decided by the government. It may be based on a wider policy for regional dispersion of industries.

Other Factors

Several other factors have to be assessed before reaching a location decision: ease in coping with environmental pollution, labor situation, climatic conditions, and general living conditions.

Site Selection

Once the broad location is chosen, attention needs to be focused on the selection of a specific site. Two or three alternative sites must be considered and evaluated with respect to cost of land and cost of site preparation and development.

Timing Tactics

It is imperative on the part of any firm that strategic planners and top managers work for finding the best timing strategies to flood the market with products. This may assume significance as many players worldwide have followed the path of first mover advantage to be derived from timing tactics. Prominent amongst the few are Intel, Apple, Philips, etc. However there are equal success stories of not having the first mover advantage. We can always look at Toyota as a good example of never entering a market on the basis of a first mover advantage. However, speeding up the time needed to innovate new products and getting them to market faster than competitors needs appropriate timing tactics.

Porter's Framework of Competitive Strategies

Michael Porter introduced generic strategies like focus, cost leadership, cost differentiation to reduce the uncertainties of the competitive environment. He also suggested the study of different components of strategic management such as the environment in which the company operates through his 'five forces' theory.

Porter in his book Competitive Strategy (1980) addressed the issue of how companies sustain their competitive advantage. Another book by Porter 'The Competitive Advantage of Nations' (1990) is major body of work on competitiveness and economic development. The ideas in the book and a series of other publications continue to guide economic policy throughout the world.

Porter's important contributions to strategic management include the 'Five force model,' the 'value chain', and the concept of 'generic strategies'. According to his 'five forces model', the nature and degree of competition in an industry depends on five forces: the threat of new entrants, the bargaining power of suppliers, the threat of substitute products, and the rivalry between existing players. To determine a strategic plan for growth in such a volatile business environment, and organization must understand how these forces operate in the industry and affect the company-specific situation.

Michael Porter recommended the use of his 'Five Forces Model' to study the different elements that comprised strategic management, such as the environment in which the company operates. Generic strategies such as cost leadership, focus and cost differentiation were introduced by Michael Porter with an aim to reduce the uncertainties of the competitive environment.

Porter also authored the books Competitive Strategy (1980) and The Competitive Advantage of Nations (1990), in which he Porter discussed the issue of sustaining competitive advantage and economic development and competitiveness

CORE COMPETENCE-CONCEPT, IMPORTANCE, BUILDNG AND USE

'We do not serve any markets; we create markets'- Akio Morita of Sony

In these changing times, cost can no longer give a firm a sustainable competitive advantage. Similarly brining a product early to the market will not enhance the competitive position of the firm in a remarkable way. Hence there is need for reinventing existing competitive space or creating entirely new competitive scope.

Alternative View of Corporate Strategy

In the past, small companies from Japan have challenged much large, richer companies from the US. How could there firms with meager resources challenge corporate giants?

For example: Canon challenging Xerox, Matsushita challenging Philips, and Honda challenging GM/FORD.

According to Gary Hamel and C.K. Prahalad:

1. The challengers have the ability to find new ways to accomplish more with less.
2. The challenges are driven by much more than short term financial goals.
3. Managers of these companies are driven by amazingly ambitious goals that go beyond typical strategic plans.
4. The challengers continue to create new forms of competitive advantages and rewrite the rules of engagement.

So what dynamic forces are at work in these organizations? Researches by the authors have revealed the following:

1. The challengers made substantial commitments to particular skill areas such as optical media, financial engineering and miniaturization, far before the markets for the end products emerged.
2. Senior managers in these organization view competition as a race to build competencies rather than a necessary evil to gain market share.
3. These teams are capable of imagining products, services and entire industries that belong only to the future.
4. Managers in these firms spend less time thinking about how to position the firm in the existing competitive space and more time on how to create fundamentally new competitive space?

How do the revolutionaries gain exclusive foresight? How is it possible to imagine markets when the products do not exist?

Current theories of strategy and organization shy away from answering these questions. These current theories rarely throw light upon what is necessary to create a framework of the future, much less make it happen. Existing views on strategy provides the framework for tracking relative competitive advantage, but fail to capture aspects of competence building. Firms have to be convinced that if they will not spare a thought for the future, they have no chance to determine what the future will be like.

Competitive Strategy as a Stretch

Companies often concentrate on resources than resourcefulness. But meeting the future in a position of strength depends more on resourcefulness than on resources. Resourcefulness stems from a deeply felt sense of purpose, a broadly shared dream, and a truly inspiring view of the future. It rarely arises from an elegantly structured strategic architecture. As such to use competitive strategy as a stretch, a firm needs to have:

- Strategic intent
- Sense of direction
- Sense of discovery
- Sense of destiny

Competitive Strategy as Leverage

Using scarce resources to maximum benefit. It is used outmaneuver rather than overpower the opposition.

Resource scarcity led to tactical creativity. For example General Motors invested billions of dollars in automation. But the firm's ability to make strategic investments completely outpaced its ability to absorb new technology, retrain workers, rejuvenate supplier relationships and discard managerial orthodoxies.

Resource leverage can be realized in five ways:

1. Concentrating resources on key strategic goals. Concentrating can be by Converging, focusing and targeting. Examples: PepsiCo
2. Efficiently accumulating resources. By data mining and borrowing. For instance, Sony commercialized the transistor and the charge coupled device technologies pioneered by AT&T s Bell laboratories.
3. By complementing resources to create more value and by blending and balancing. Both GM and FORD spend more than Honda to develop engine related technologies such as combustion engineering, electronic control etc., and attained leadership position, but they are behind Honda in terms of all-round engine performance, because they were not so good at blending technologies.
4. Conserving the resources by recycling, co-opting, protection. Example: P&G and Unilever recycling their brands.

5. By recovering: Minimizing the time between expenditure and payback. For instance, faster product development times.

Concept of Core Competence-C.K. Prahalad and Gary Hamel's Views

Study of GTE & NEC

Fact file-

GTE – 1989-$ 9.98 billion USD; 1988 - $16.46 billion USD

NEC- 1980 - $ 3.8 billion USD; 1988 - $ 21.89 billion USD

During this period in 1988, GTE divested some of its business and closed down a few. In the same period NEC emerged as a leader in the semiconductor business and diversified into mobile phones/facsimile and laptop computers.

Prahalad and Hamel are of the opinion that while in the short run a company's competitiveness depends on the price/performance attributes of its products, in the long run competitiveness depends on the ability to build core competencies faster than competitors and at a lower cost.

According to Prahalad and Hamel, this was because NEC conceived of itself in terms of core competencies and GTE did not. Prahalad and Hamel are of the opinion that while in the short run a company's competitiveness depends on the price/performance attributes of its products, in the long run competitiveness depends on the ability to build core competencies faster than competitors and at a lower cost. Insight/ foresight competencies enable a company to learn facts that create first mover advantages. For instance, invovation-3M, miniaturization-Sony.

A frontline execution competency refers to the unique ability to deliver products and service whose quality equal to the best that could have been produced under ideal circumstances. Example: McDonald's

Concept of Core Competency-Krishna Palepu and Tarun Khanna's Views

In their HBR article 'Why Focused Strategies May be Wrong of Emerging Markets' the authors argued that focus or emphasis on core businesses may not be the right strategy in emerging markets. They mentioned that focus is good for western countries where there are institutions that support their business activities.

But may such institutions are absent in emerging markets. Companies must adapt their strategies to fit a country's product, capital, labor markets and regulatory system.

According to Khanna and Palepu, diversified business groups are better suited to developing countries like the Chaebols of Korea, the business houses of India and the Groups of Latin America.

Strategic Analysis and Choice

Strategic analysis is done at corporate and business levels using tools such as the BCG (Boston Consulting Group) Growth-Share Matrix, and the GE Nine-Cell Planning Grid to examine each business as a separate entity and as a contribution to the organization's total business portfolio. In this unit, you will learn that strategic analysis offers three potential advantages. First, it encourages the framing of good strategies at the business unit level. Second, it provides a neutral basis for resource allocation. Third, it leads to better implementation of strategy because intensified focus and objectivity increase the commitment of workers at all levels. Once business units are classified into invest, hold, and harvest categories, a SWOT analysis is employed to identify grand strategy options at the business level.

CORPORATE LEVEL ANALYSIS

BCG Growth-Share Matrix

BCG Growth-Share Matrix is widely used in corporate strategic analysis. This matrix helps in analyzing likely 'generators' and optimum 'using' of corporate resources. Organizations have to take decisions regarding the allocation of resources between competing business units. However, an organization is required to take decisions based on some fundamental criteria. The Boston Consulting Group came up with a model for managing a portfolio of different business units (or major product lines), in the 1970s. This matrix takes into consideration, the growth rate of the market and the relative market share of the business unit. It is important to pay attention to the market growth rate because it is a crucial factor that determines whether the organization should stay in a particular industry or not. Rapid growth and maximum returns are possible for a firm only in booming industries. Hence, it is prudent for returns are possible for a firm only in booming industries. Hence, it is prudent for an organization to enter and continue to operate in a growing industry. High market share gives some special benefits to the organization such as economies of scale and bargaining power in relation to buyers and sellers. The BCG growth-share matrix displays the positions of business units on a graph of the market growth rate against their market share relative to competitors.

Resources can be allocated to business units on the basis of their classification into categories. Business units are classified into four categories, namely cash cows, stars, question marks, and dogs.

- **Cash Cows**

These business units hold a large market share in a mature and slow-growing industry. They have a strong business position and negligible investment requirements and hence the returns from these businesses are often more than their investment requirements. Organizations often tap their cash cows in order to draw out resources required elsewhere in the organization.

- **Stars**

These business units have a large market share in the fast growing market or industries. Firms need to invest in stars as the industry is still emerging and the market is also growing. Often, the investment requirements of stars are greater than the revenues they generate. But once the industry reaches the stage of maturity, the stars hardly need any investment and become major sources of revenue for the firms.

- **Question Marks**

These business units have a small market share in a high growth market. They demand significant investment because their cash needs are high, a norm in a growing industry. As the market grows rapidly, acquiring market share is easier than in a mature market. However, the stage of growth in the industry is characterized by a lot of uncertainty that results from changes in technologies, distribution channels, and the players themselves. Hence, there are only a few question marks that are able to grow into stars.

- **Dogs**

These business units have low market share in an intensely competitive mature industry characterized by low profits. A dog does not need much of investment, but it ties up capital that could be invested in industries with better returns. Hence, organizations concentrate on recovering as much as possible from these units in terms of returns on investment and often undertake ruthless cost cutting. Unless there is larger purpose in keeping such units, an organization should divest of dogs at the earliest.

However, recent research suggests that well-managed dogs can have a positive effect on the organization, and be highly reliable revenue generators. These well- managed dogs have a narrow business focus, concentrate on high product quality and moderate prices, have strong control over costs, and advertise only to a limited extent. Though these units can generate surplus returns, yet the possibility of being transformed into a cash cow does not exist.

Though the BCG matrix provides a framework for allocation resources among different business units and allow one to compare many business units, it criticized for oversimplification. For example, the relation between market share and profitability is questionable, and the emphasis on improving marketing share may lead the organization is a direction which does not meet its objectives.

BCG Growth – Share Matrix

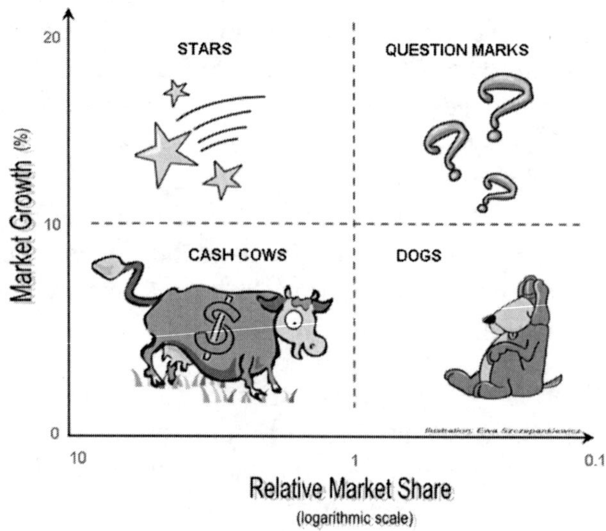

The GE Nine- Cell Planning Grid

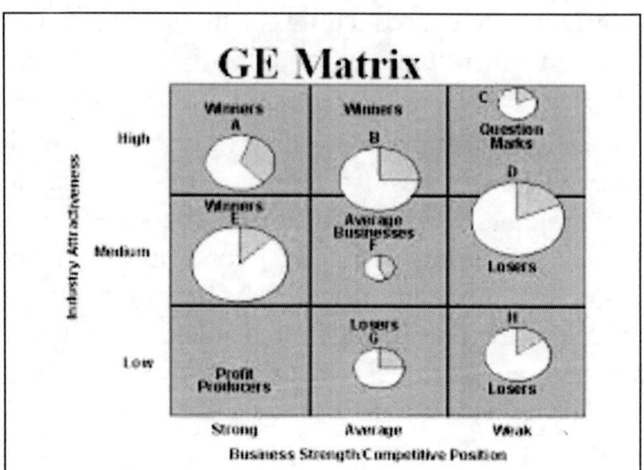

The grid as shown above is an adaption of the BCG approach and was popularized by General Electric. Hence, the name GE Nine-Cell Planning Grid. This grid makes an effort to overcome some of the limitations of the BCG matrix. The GE grid deploys multiple factors to measure business strength and industry attractiveness. It uses factors such as market share, profit margin, customer and market knowledge, ability to compete, technology, competitive position and management caliber to asses' business strength. It also gives due importance to industry attractiveness, factors such as market growth, competition, seasonality and cyclical qualities, size and industry profitability, economies of scale, technology and various social, environmental, legal and human factors. Next, the position of the business is determined by calculating subjective values of the two dimensions of the grid.

The strategist first identifies the factors contributing to the industry attractiveness. Next, he assigns weights to each industry attractiveness factor based on its perceived importance relative to the other attractiveness factors. Favourable to unfavourable future conditions are forecasted and rated bases on a 0-1 scale. Thus, the strategist obtains a weighted composite score for the business's overall industry attractiveness as shown in Table

Industry Attractiveness Factor

Industry Attractiveness	**Weight**	**Rating***	**Score Factor**
Market size	20	0.5	10.0
Projected market growth	35	1.0	35.0
Technological requirements	15	0.5	7.5
Concentration (a few large competitors)	30	0	0
Political and regulatory factors	Must be restrictive	-	-
Total	**100**		**52.5**

A similar procedure is followed in assessing the business strength as shown in Table

Assessing Business Strength

Business Strength	**Weight**	**Rating**	**Score Factor**
Relative market share	20	0.5	10
Production			
Capacity	10	1.0	10
Efficiency	10	1.0	10
Location	20	0	0
Technological Capability	20	0.5	10
Market			
Sales organization	15	1.0	15
Promotion advantage	5	0	0
Total	**100**		**55**

High= 1.0; Medium = 0.5; Low=0.0

Once the comprehensive score has been calculated, the scores are classified into ratings such as high, medium, or low in terms of the projected strength of the business and the projected attractiveness of the industry. Next, the business units are classified into three categories. First, invest/grow; second, invest selectively and mange for earning; and third, harvest or divest for resources.

Business units classified as invest/grow are given the same preference of stars as given in the BCG matrix. Resources are then allocated to pursue growth-oriented strategies. Organizations are encouraged to divest from these business to finance other business. Business classified in the selectivity/ earnings category are treated either are cash cows or as question marks.

Hofer's Product/ Market Evolution

For identifying strategic choices, an analytical model was designed by Charles Hofer which consists of a three-by-five matrix, wherein business units are classified on the basis of two parameters-the product market evolution of the units, and their competitive positions. The relative size of the respective industries is represented by circles and the relative market share of the concerned business is shown by shaded parts of the circle. Stages in product/market evolution are plotted on the vertical axis of the matrix divided into five segments. E.g., developments, growth, shake out, maturity to saturation and decline. The competitive position is plotted along the horizontal axis in three segments- strong, average, and weak.

Find below an illustration of Hofer's matrix.

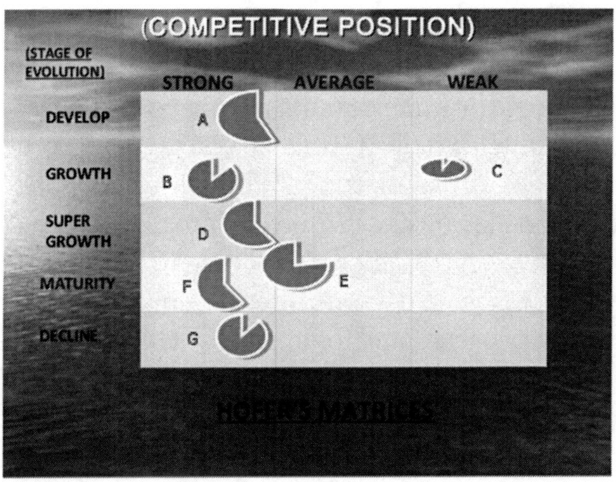

Hofer's Matrix

Strategic approaches for any particular business unit may be considered depending upon the stage of its product market evolution and competitive strength. If the market share of a business is large and it is in the development or growth stage, it would require more resources to be developed to develop its competitive position. It has the potential to be in the 'Star category' as in BCG matrix. For a business in the development stage having low market share, a strategy to improve the market share is called for. However management should consider a divestment strategy if any business with low market share belongs to a relatively small industry, even if it is in the development or growth stage. Resources available as a result of divestment may be redeployed in other business units with strong competitive position.

Shell's Directional Policy Matrix (DPM) Model

This model for understanding strategy choice was developed by Roy Dutch Shell. It aims at placing each product/market unit (SBU) on a matrix according to its rating based on two variables-business sector prospects, and company's competitive capabilities. The various zones of the matrix are thus associated with different combinations of 'business sector prospects' and 'company's competitive strength or weakness', The type of strategy or resource allocation which is appropriate is suggested for the product /market units falling in the respective zones.

The application of this model hinges on the identification of two sets of criteria.

i. Criteria by which the prospects for business sector may be judged to be favorable or unfavorable

ii. Criteria by which the company's competitive position may be judged to be strong or weak

Types of Strategy of SBUs Falling in the Various Zones

Business Sector Prospects

		Business Sector Prospects		
Company's Competitive Capabilities		**Unattractive**	**Average**	**Attractive**
	Weak	Disinvest	Phased Withdrawal	Double or quit
	Average	Phased withdrawal	Custodial growth	Try harder
	Strong	Cash generation	Growth Leader	leader

In the Table, of the Directional Policy matrix, the types of strategy for SBUs falling in the various zones are indicated. The keywords used are briefly explained below:

- **Leader:** The SBU, which is in an enviable position of being the largest producer with the lowest unit costs and a superior technical position, may be regarded as leader in the business sector. In such a position, the product needs to have absolute priority of support by way of resource allocation to hold the market share.
- **Try harder:** This position indicates attractive sector prospects but average competitive capability. Products located in this zone ought to be provided with necessary resources so as to move them to positions of equality.
- **Double or quit:** Products in this zone with attractive sector prospects but weak competitive ability should be governed by discrete choice of strategy. Out of these products may be found some with bright future. The strategy should be to select and back up the right product.
- **Growth:** Product in this zone with average to strong competitive ability (being one among two to four major competitors) and with at least average sector prospect are

suited for growth strategy support by adequate production capacity and product R&D.

- **Custodial:** Product is located in the custodial zone of the matrix when the company has competitive ability or sector prospect or both in combination. The company must bear with the situation and make good the overall position with the help of other product units.
- **Cash generation:** With a strong competitive position in a sector which is unattractive from the point of view of business prospects, a company may be able to earn satisfactory profits and generate cash.
- **Phased withdrawal:** The strategy of phased withdrawal is indicated where a company is in an average-to weak competitive position in a low-growth (unattractive) business sector with little prospect of generating substantial cash. Attempts should be made in such a situation to realize the value of assets and invest the money in more profitable business segments.
- **Disinvest:** SBU's running is losses with uncertain cash flows are located in this zone. A divestment strategy is called for in this case so that resources thereby released may be put to better use.

INDUSTRY LEVEL ANALYSIS

Porter's Five Force Model

Effective formulation of strategy requires a clear understanding of competition. Competition in an industry is determined not only by existing competitors but also by other market forces such as customers, suppliers, potential entrants, and the existence of substitute products. Understanding the level of competition is important because the level of profits depends to a large extent upon the level of competition. The strategist's goal is to position the firm in such a way that it is not vulnerable to the attacks of competitors. The position should give the firm enough space to defend itself confidently. Given this, the need to study the underlying sources of competitive pressures is obvious. Understanding the sources of competition can help the firm to gauge its own strengths and weaknesses, and to perceive the trends in the industry so that it can position itself optimally for the best returns. The 'Five Forces Model' is a framework which has been developed by Michael E. Porter of the Harvard Business School to assist managers in analyzing the business environment. The five forces that play a crucial role in shaping a company's future are as follows:

i. Bargaining power of customers
ii. Threat posed by substitute products
iii. Bargaining power of suppliers
iv. Threat posed by new entrants
v. Competition among existing firms

These five forces are discussed in detail as follows:

1. Bargaining power of Customers

Customers are the ones who buy products from the sellers. However, they are not always the final users of the product. For example, for Procter and Gamble the direct buyers of its detergents are wholesalers and retailers. Bulk buyers such as supermarkets often have greater bargaining power i.e., they can ask the supplier company for prices lower than single customers or small retailers. If buyers are in a weak bargaining position than the supplier, the supplying company can hike prices and make profits on that basis. Thus, the bargaining power of buyers is one of the factors in industry-level strategic analysis. Porter says that buyers are powerful under the following circumstances:

- When the suppliers are many, and the buyers are a few and large.
- When the buyers purchase in large quantities.
- When the supplier's business banks on the buyers for the lion's share of its total orders.

- When buyers can force prices to go down by switching orders between supplying companies. This is because they pit companies against each other.
- When it is economically feasible for the buyers to purchase the input from several companies at a time.
- When, as a result of the threat, the buyers can attend to their own requirements through vertical integration, forcing the prices to go down in the process.

For example, the buyers of auto components are powerful. In the US, the buyers are General Motors, Ford and Chrysler. There are numerous suppliers of auto components. So, to keep the buyers loyal to them, auto component suppliers must provide quality products to their buyers.

2. Bargaining power of suppliers

The suppliers' power to bargain influences the profits earned by the company. This occurs when the suppliers determine the price that the customers or buyers must pay for the product. Suppliers are powerful under the following circumstances:

- When the product that they sell has few substitutes and is important to the purchasing company or buyer.
- When no single industry is a major customer for the suppliers.
- When products in the industry are differentiated to such an extent that they are not easily substitutable and it is costly for a buyer to switch from one supplier to another.
- To raise prices, the supplier can use the threat of vertically integrating forward into the industry and competing directly with the buying company.
- The buying companies cannot use the threat of vertically integrating backward and supplying their own needs as a means to reduce input prices.

One example of a powerful supplier is Microsoft, the world's largest provider of operation software. Manufactures of computers, laptop, etc., are almost totally depended on Microsoft to run their PCs as it is the most popular and reliable software used universally all over the world.

3. Threat posed by substitute products

Companies in the coffee industry are restricted. If coffee prices are hiked, customers have the option of switching over to tea of soft drinks, which are its substitutes.

A close substitute is a potential threat to the company's product. The existence of a substitute limited the price which can be charged for a product and therefore the profitability of the company.

4. Threat posed by new entrants

Generally new entrants into any industry tend capture the market share with their new capacity. As a result, there are more players and more competition. The situation can lead to price wars, which can result in falling returns. This decline in profitability becomes a problem for the new entrants too. That is why new entrants to an industry often take the 'acquisitions' route. There are certain barriers that determine a firm's ability to enter an industry. The six barriers are as follows.

i. Government policies

ii. Capital requirements

iii. Cost disadvantage irrespective of size

iv. Economies of scale

v. Product differentiation

vi. Access to distribution channels

5. Competition among existing firms

Intense competition is referred to as rivalry. It occurs in an industry when one business or many businesses try to increase their market share.

Rivalry may lead to price wars, advertising battles, launch of new products and increased customer services and warranties. Some firms gain the upper hand through intense rivalry, while their competitors suffer a fall in market share. The intensity of rivalry depends upon many factors. Rivalry is usually intense when there are many competitors of similar size. Slowdowns in industrial growth also make firms keen to grab each other's market share. A lack of differentiation among the products of the players in the industry also leads to intense competition. The absence of switching cost can lead to an unstable market place. In the paper and aluminum industries, manufactures often resort to underpricing to avoid spoilage of the goods. It is difficult for firms to move out of certain industries, because of their fixed investments. Thus, a variety of factors, ranging from exit barriers to the loyalty of old players the industry, despite low returns, increases the intensity of competition in an industry.

Analysis of the Indian Pharma Industry Using Porter's Model

Present-day business operates in immensely competitive conditions. However, in conditions of a perfect competition profits completely cease to exist presenting the impossibility of the scenario since no business is operative in such conditions and company's strives to create a competitive advantage to succeed amid competition. Michael Porter developed the popular five-force model, which is applied here to the Indian Pharma industry.

Porter's Five Forces

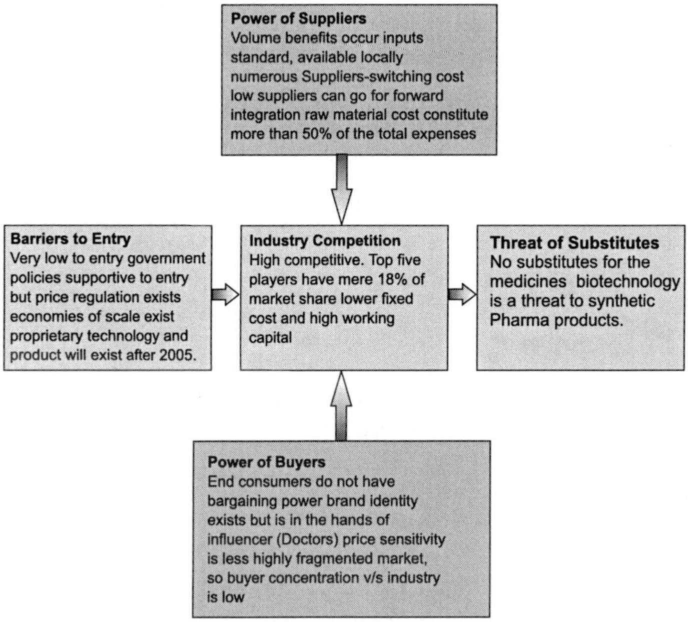

Competition in the Industry

The pharmaceutical industry is exposed to intense competition with about 10,000 companies.

The top companies have only six per cent of the market share while the top five companies possess only eighteen per cent of the share. There is an immense growth potential in the segment which increases rivalry, as various companies' entry the industry. While the fixed cost requirement is low, the need for working capital is high. The fixed asset turnover, (one of the measures of fixed cost requirements), reveals that in big companies the ratio ranges from 3.5 to 4 times, which is even higher for small companies. Small companies, which are limited to specific areas, have the advantage of a better distribution channel. A significant factor is that the pharmaceutical industry possesses an unalterable market and its progress follows the economic progress of the country

(1.2 times average in India). But although there has been a growth over the past years, there has been no value growth. Differentiation provides competitive advantage in industries but in the pharmaceutical industry, product differentiation is not possible since India follows process patents, with laws aiding imitators. Thus, cost competitiveness gains an advantage over product differentiation. Nonetheless, eminent companies including Pfizer and Glaxo have emerged as respectable brands marketing a niche in the industry, functioning as tools of product differentiation.

Buyer power

In the Pharma industry buyers lack control over the purchase of a product, as medicines are purchased on prescriptions. A buyer's power implies the influence customers have on the pricing of a product but in the pharmaceutical industry no such power is wielded on consumers. It is the government which regulates prices implemented by the NPA (National Pharmaceutical Authority).

Supplier power

The pharmaceutical industry relies on various organic chemicals. The chemical industry too, is competitive and highly fragmented. The suppliers hold little authority over chemical companies, who can change suppliers without threat of high costs. Nonetheless, the supplier can integrate into a Pharma company. Companies including Orchid Chemical and Sashum Chemicals have transformed from chemical companies to pharmaceutical companies.

Control of access

Entry in the Pharma industry is unrestricted due a low capital requirement and an easy distribution network, owing to the limitation of sales in India. It becomes essential to develop brand awareness and a franchisee amongst medical professionals for better future prospects. Another obstacle in the establishment of new industries is the quality regulations by the government. The new patent regulations will further restrict entry, but as the demand for pharmaceuticals will always remain consistent, new industries are more likely to enter the market.

Risk of alternatives

One of the primary benefits of the Pharma industry is its highly promising future prospects. Competition in the industry is facilitated by limitless possibilities. Nonetheless, in the past few years, the development of biotechnology can be viewed as potential danger to the Pharma industry.

Analysis of the Telecom Sector Using Porter's Model

Danger of new entrants

The telecom industry is impeded by exorbitant costs required to incorporate the high fixed costs. The danger of newly established competitors increases as the capital markets flourish. But a lack of a telecom license limits entry to some extent. In the US, entry in the telecom Industry is regulated by the Federal Communications Commission, even for established industries. Limitations in the percentage of 'good' radio spectrum also regulate mobile voice and data applications. Also, the technical skills and management experience is limited impeding market entry.

Supplier control

Telecom equipment suppliers have little control over telecom operators, although hi-tech broadband switching equipment, fibre-optic cables, mobile handsets and billing software remain at the disposal of suppliers without which operators will fail to transmit data. There is a large supplier market, including key players like Nortel, Lucent, Cisco, Nokia, Alcatel, Ericsson and Tellabs. Thus, an abundant supply pool reduces the supplier power which is further curtailed by a scarcity in available talent, specifically those with an upgraded knowledge of current technologies.

Buyer control

Immense competition in the telecom industry ensures a rise in buyer control. Basic services are commodified and customers make decisions based on reliable services offered at low prices. Varying markets also affect buyer control. The customers may range from individual users to large scale industries and multinational corporations such as an ISP like America Online. Thus, the switching-costs can have a major impact on large corporations relying on increasingly customized services.

Scope for alternatives

The launch of cable TV and satellite links have had a detrimental effect on the telecom industry, Large-scale business and corporations including the railways and the power corporation are employing the Internet and satellite links substituting telecom networking. The latest hazard faced by telecom operators is posed by the internet. Internet is fast-replacing other means of telecommunication, carving a niche for itself in the domain of 'Internet telephony'. ISP's not only cut costs but provide easy accessibility becoming an effective mode of communication.

Rising Competition

The late 1990's witnessed a rise in the telecom industry, owing to industry de-regulation and increasing market receptivity. Phone services constitute the category of essential services so competitors must aim at a larger market share within affordable prices and quality services, entailing a decrement in the profit margin of the industry. Further, the scope for liquidation is negated owing to highly specialized equipment including networks and billing systems which is rendered infertile in case of another use.

QUALITATIVE FACTORS IN STRATEGIC CHOICE

Strategy formulation, according to Henry Mintzberg, is interplay of three basic forces:

1. A dynamic environment that changes continuously but irregularly with frequent discontinuities and wide swings in the rate of change.
2. The operation system of the organization which seeks to stabilize its activities despite the characteristics of the environment it serves.
3. The role of leadership mediating between the two forces so as to maintain stability of the organization's operating system while at the same time adapting it to the environmental change.
4. Strategic choice involves selecting from among several alternatives the most appropriate strategy which will best serve the enterprise objectives. The choice takes place within a frame of reference consisting of different elements, and the choice made is the product of interaction of the elements in the frame of reference.

Alvar Elbing has distinguished between seven categories of such elements.

1. Accumulated knowledge base
2. Decision making processes
3. Assumptions about cause and effect
4. Human needs
5. Past experiences
6. Expectations
7. Culture and Values

According to William Glueck, strategic choices are made in the light of four selection factors:

i. Managerial perceptions of external dependence
ii. Managerial attitudes towards risk
iii. Managerial awareness of past enterprise strategies
iv. Managerial power relationships and organization structure

Similar factors have been suggested by other writers but classified differently for analytical purposes. Indeed the factors which may influence the choice of strategy are many, some of which may be constraints limiting the scope of choice.

Factors Influencing the Strategic Choice

The important factors influencing the strategic choice are:

1. External constraints

The survival and prosperity of a firm depend largely on its interaction with the elements or units in the environment-shareholders, customers, suppliers, competitors, the government and the society at large. These elements constitute the eternal constraints, and flexibility in the choice of strategy is often governed by the extent and degree of the firm's dependence on the elements.

2. Intra-organizational forces and managerial power-relations

Within an organization major decisions are often influenced by the power play among different interest groups. Strategic decisions are no exception. Research finding have thrown considerable light on the impact of managerial power-relations on strategic choice.

3. Values and preferences and managerial attitudes towards risk

The role of value systems in decision-making by managers is well established. While evaluating the strategic alternatives, different executives may take different positions because of differences in their personal values and the consequent weighing of key factors.

4. Impact of past strategy

The choice of current strategy may be influenced by the earlier strategy for a variety of reasons. Since past strategies are usually the starting point in the formulation of new strategies, some alternatives may not be explored as thoroughly as might be otherwise expected or certain alternatives may not be considered at all.

5. The constraints in choice strategy

The time dimension of strategic choice is another factor in the strategic decision process that may be of considerable significance. Four elements of time dimension may be worth noting. These are: (i) Time pressure (ii) Time frame (iii) Time horizon, and (iv) Timing of the decision.

6. Information constraints

A crucial factor in the choice of strategy is the availability of information. It is on the basis of relevant data and information that executives are likely to make a decision. The degree of uncertainty and risk depends upon the amount of information that executives depends upon the amount of information that is available to the decision-maker.

7. Competitor's reaction

Consideration of competitor's reaction to any strategic option is often required in weighing strategic choices. Suppose the option being considered by a company is an aggressive strategy challenging a near-equal competitor. It is quite possible that the competitor would adopt a counter-strategy so as to with stand the aggressive strategy of the initiating company. It would be unrealistic for the company not to consider the possibility. The management must take into account the likelihood of the reaction, the competitor's capability to react, and its impact on the strategic choice.

FACTORS AFFECTING STRATEGIC CHOICE

Strategic refers to the decision to adopt one of possible alternative strategies. The decision process becomes relatively simple when the analysis clearly identifies a superior strategy or when the current strategy clearly meets the company objectives for the future. When different alternatives promise similar payoffs, the decision making process becomes judgmental and difficult because the decision makers are confronted with viable alternative rather than a clear-cut choice. Under such circumstances, various factors influence the choice. Some of these factors are as follows:

- **Role of past Strategy:** The process of strategic choice begins with a review of past strategy. Often, a firm's strategists are also the architects of strategies used earlier. Owing to their familiarity with and commitment to past strategy, both lower-level managers and top-level managers exhibit a preference for continuity. This is probably the reason why firms sometimes replace key executives when the performance of the firm proves to be inadequate for an extended period, because replacing them lessens the influence of past strategies and provides more options for the future. On the other hand, the more successful the strategy becomes, the harder it is to replace it with a new one, even under changed circumstances.
- **Attitude towards risk:** The firm's attitude towards risk influences the range of strategic choices available. Some organizations have a strong aversion to risk, while others are eager risk-takers. The range and diversity of the strategic choice expands when these attitudes are adequately controlled before strategic choices are made. In risk-oriented organizations, high-risk strategies are accepted and even seen as desirable.
- **Competitive reaction:** Organizations have to take into consideration the reactions of competitors while making strategic choices. If a firm chooses an aggressive strategy that directly challenges a key competitor, then that competitor is sure to launch a counter strategy. Keeping this point in view, the management of the initiating firm must consider aspects such as the capacity of the competitor to react and the probable impact of the reaction on the chosen strategy.
- **Degree of firm's external dependence:** A comprehensive strategy is meant to ensure a high

level of performance in the external environment. The various components of the external environment are as follows:

- Suppliers
- Government
- Competitors
- Unions

A major constraint when making a strategic choice is the extent of influence of environmental elements on a firm's decision. The greater the firm's dependence on external factors, the lower will be the range and flexibility of its strategic choice.

- **Values and preferences:** An important basis of strategic choice lies in the background, needs, desires and values of the owners and managers. The manager and owner's attitudes and their influence are seen and felt clearly in smaller companies. These factors also affect large organizations, depending on the amount of actual control in the hands of one or a few individuals. Although the extent of influence varies, the characteristics of owners and managers invariably play a part in the process of strategic choice.

FOUR KEY QUESTIONS

The four key questions of corporate strategy are as follows:

1. What is the overall rationale of the corporate parent in terms of how it envisages itself as enhancing the value created by the business units for its shareholders/ stakeholders?
2. What is the logic of the mix of business units in the corporate portfolio and how does this make sense in terms of the corporate rationale?
3. Is the extent and type of diversity of the corporation sensible given the corporate rationale and logic of the portfolio?

4. How does the corporate parent and business units interact; in particular, how does the centre seek to manage business units?

STRATEGIC ANALYSIS

Strategic analysis is done at the corporate and business levels. Tools such as BCG Growth-Share Matrix and GE Nine-Cell Planning Grid are used at the corporate level to examine each business as a separate entity and as a contributor to the organization's total business portfolio. This analysis offers three potential advantages. Firstly, it encourages the framing of good strategies at the business unit level; secondly, it provides a neutral basis for resource allocation; and thirdly, it leads to better implementation of strategy as the intensified focus and objectivity increases the commitment of workers at all levels. Once business units are classified into invest, hold and harvest categories, a SWOT analysis is performed to identify the appropriate strategy option at the business level. These have been discussed in detail in Units 6 and 7. Here we shall discuss the Arthur D Little Life Cycle Approach.

Arthur D little's Life Cycle Approach

The highly respected Arthur D Little (ADL) consulting Company developed the ADL Matrix in the closing years of the 1970s. This matrix assists in developing a strategy built on industry maturity, or the stage at which the industry is in its lifecycle; and competitive position, or the strength of its strategic position. For example, business units having newly developing product lines and strong market presences would prefer to thrust their position forward aggressively and gain as high market share as possible. However, a business enterprise that has a leading competitive position in a declining market would not favour such a strategy. It would rather endeavor to maintain its present market position in the deteriorating industry and expend its energies on gaining a foothold in new, emerging markets.

All these distinct needs are addressed by the ADL Matrix that recommends certain general strategies that apply to various combinations of industry maturity and competitive position.

Industry Maturity

Industry maturity (also known as the industry life cycle) can be divided into the following categories:

1. **Embryonic-** This introductory stage is characterized by minimum competition, swift market growth, high prices, high investment and new technology.

2. **Growth-** Sales figures rise and the market gains in strength with only a few (if any) competitors existing. The company gains the rewards of introducing new products into the market.

3. **Mature-** The customer base is well-established, and the market and the market share are quite stable. The number of competitors is significantly high and considerable energy is spent on differentiating the company from the competitors.

4. **Aging-** The demand declines and business begin to abandon the market. The struggle for market share among the remaining competitors proves to be very costly, and business continues to leave or consolidate until the market dies.

Competitive Position

The following are the different categories of competitive position:

1. **Dominant-** A rare and usually short-lived position, in this stage, the competition is at its minimum, as a consequence of a very strong foothold in the market (e.g., Microsoft) or due to the introduction of a new and innovative product into the market.

2. **Strong-** Irrespective of what they competitors do, the market share is stable and strong.

3. **Favorable-** The business benefits form competitive advantages in certain market segments. But the number of

competitors is also high, as a result of which the company has to constantly endeavor to sustain the advantage.

4. Tenable- The position of the business is small in the overall market. The market share has its basis in a strong geographic location, some product differentiation, or a niche of some sort. The stronger competitors build their products and define clear competitive advantages, and thus overtake the business' market share.

5. Weak- The market share continually declines and the business line is found to be too small to sustain its profitability.

Application of the Life Cycle Approach

The application of the life cycle approach involves the follows steps:

1. Identifying each line of business: Using criteria such as common rivals, customers, sustainability, prices, quality/style, and divestment or liquidation

2. Assessing the life cycle stage of each business: Based on cash flows or profitability, investment and business market share

3. Identifying the competitive position of the firm: As dominant, strong, favorable, tenable or weak

4. Identifying the strategy for the SBU: On the basis of competitive position and life cycle stage.

5. Assigning a strategic thrust to the natural strategy

6. Selection of one of the twenty-four generic strategies.

PROFIT IMPACT OF MARKET STRATGIES

During the period in which the GE-Nine Cell Planning Grid was developed, another more quantitative approach to portfolio planning was also developed under the aegis of the profit Impact of Market Strategies (PIMS) programme. By the mid-1970s, PIMS had data on 620 SBUs from fifty-seven diversified companies. This data was used to understand the determinants of returns on investment. This was done by regressing historical returns on variables such as R&D expenditure, marketing, investment intensity, product quality and market share. The regression established benchmarks for the potential performance of SBUs and pointed out their characteristics, which were then compared with the actual performance.

ANSOFF'S PRODUCT MARKET MATRIX

The debate on whether a firm should gamble on its ability to build distinctive competence to pursue opportunities continued throughout the 1960s. This was mainly because during the 1960s, corporate strategies were heavily tilted towards growth and diversification. According to Theodore Levitt, firms should not be too focused on delivering products on the basis of distinctive competence. Instead, they should consciously serve the customer. According to him, companies do not succeed when their product fail to adapt to the changing tastes and needs of consumers, when their products fail to adapt to the changing tastes and needs of consumers, when they fail to develop new marketing initiatives and when they fail to keep pace with product develop in complementary industries.

However, according to Ansoff, developing new products that were not in keeping with a firm's distinctive competence entailed unnecessary risks. He argued that the first question that a company should ask was whether there was a 'common thread' between the new product and the existing products of the company. According to him, a common thread was the commitment of a firm or its mission to take advantage of an existing requirement in the market as a whole. He clarified that although a customer may sometimes be erroneously identified as the common thread, actually, s/he would often have a variety of distinct needs or product missions. Therefore, he came up with certain categories to define the common thread of a firm's corporate/business strategy.

Product/Market Matrix of Ansoff

	Present Product	**New Product**
Present Market	Market penetration	Product development
New Market	Market development	**Diversification**

- **Market Development:** The aim of the firm is to achieve growth by directing its existing products at newer segments of the market.
- **Market Penetration:** The aim of the firm is to achieve growth with existing products in its present market segments.
- **Diversification:** The aim of the firm is to diversify into new business by coming up with new products for new markets.
- **Product Development:** The aim of the firm is to develop new products directed at its existing market segments.

SUMMARY

- Strategic decisions made at the corporate level of organizations are those which significantly affect business units.
- Mergers are the integration of two or more firms on a co-equal basis. A merger between two firms operating and competing in the same business activity is known as a horizontal merger. Merging of two firms in the same industry but in different stages of the value chain is known as a vertical merger.
- When firms try to enter new markets, they often face many problems, some of which may act as barriers to entry.
- Restructuring can be defined as a strategy by which a company changes its business or financial structure.

Restructuring can happen in the form of expansions, sell-offs corporate control and changes in ownership structure.

- The choice of location and site follows an assessment of demand size and input requirements.
- In these changing times, cost can no longer give firms a sustainable competitive environment. BCG Growth-Share Matrix is widely used in corporate strategic analysis; this matrix helps in analyzing likely 'generators' and optimum 'uses' of substitute products.
- Strategic analysis is done at the corporate and business levels. Tools such as BCG Growth-Share entity and a contributor to the organizations' total business portfolio
- According to Ansoff developing new products that were not in keeping with the firm's distinctive competence entailed unnecessary risks.

KEY TERMS

- **Mergers:** integration of two or more firms on a co-equal basis.
- **Horizontal merger:** A merger between two firms operating and competing in the same business activity.
- **Vertical merger:** Merging of two firms in the same industry but in different stages of the value chain.
- **Restructuring:** A strategy by which a company changes its business or financial structure.
- **BCG Growth-share Matrix:** Widely used in corporate strategic analysis; this matrix helps in analyzing likely 'generators' and optimum 'uses' of corporate resources.
- **Market development:** The aim of the firm is to achieve growth by directing its existing market segments.

ANSWERS TO 'CHECK YOUR PROGRESS'

1. One of the 'four key questions' which form the basis for corporate level strategies is:

- What is the overall rationale of the corporate parent in terms of how it envisages itself enhancing the value created by the business units for its shareholders/stakeholders?

2. Acquisition refers to the process of gaining complete or partial control of a company by another company for some strategic reasons.
3. The reasons for cross-border mergers and acquisitions are:
   - Growth
   - Technology
   - Government Policy
   - Source of raw materials
   - Differential labor costs and productivity
4. Expansion can take place through mergers and acquisitions, tender offers or joint ventures.
5. Availability of power, transportation, water and communication should be carefully assessed before a location decision is made.
6. To use competitive strategy, a firm requires:
   - Strategic intent
   - Sense of direction
   - Sense of discovery
   - Sense of destiny
7. The five in Porter's Five Force Model are:

   i. Bargaining power of customers

   ii. Threat posed by substitute products

   iii. Bargaining power of suppliers

   iv. Threat posed by new entrants

   v. Competition among existing firms.

8. Factors affecting strategic choice are:
   - Role of past strategy
   - Attitude towards risk
   - Competitive reaction
   - Degree of firm's external dependence
   - Value and preference

QUESTIONS AND EXERCIES

Short-Answer Questions

1. Write a brief note on mergers and acquisitions.
2. What is the difference between a vertical merger and a horizontal merger?
3. List the qualitative differences between reengineering and restructuring.
4. Write short notes on site selection and timing tactics regarding corporate-level strategies?
5. Write a short note on competitive strategy as leverage?
6. Write a short note on the GE Nine-Cell Planning Grid.

Long –Answer Questions

1. Explain in detail the rationale for mergers and acquisitions
2. What are the reasons for cross-border merger and acquisitions? Elaborate.
3. Discuss in detail the concept of synergy.
4. Elaborate on the BCG Growth-Share Matrix and the GE Nine-Cell Planning Grid.
5. List and explain Porter's Five Force Model.
6. List and evaluate the factors affecting strategic choice.

FURTHER READING

Johnson,Gerry and Kevan Scholes. 1994. Exploring Corporate Strategy: Text and Cases. New Delhi: Prentice-Hall of India.

Thompson, Arthur A. and A.J.Strickland. 1997. Strategic Management: Concepts and Cases. Illinois: Irwin Professional Publishing.

Dess, Gregory G., G.T. Lumpkin and Alan B.Eisner. 2008. Strategic Management: Text and Cases. New York: McGraw-Hill/Irwin.

Pearce, John A. and Richard B. Robinson. 1999. Strategic Management. New York: McGraw-Hill.

Kazmi, Azhar. 2002. Business Policy and Strategic Management. New Delhi: Tata McGraw-Hill.

Unit 5

STRATEGY IMPLEMENTATION

INTRODUCTION

Strategy implementation involves several interrelated decisions, choices and a broad range of activities. In this Unit, we will be discussing strategy implementation in some detail. We will be looking at the differentiation and integration of strategy. Also, we will be discussing systems in strategic implementation, such as Simple, Functional, Divisional and Matrix structure. There is also a brief discussion on the strategic business unit (SBU) structure, and holding business structure.

UNIT OBJECTIVES

After going through this unit, you will be able to:

- Explain strategic implementation
- Discuss differentiation and integration of strategy
- Learn about systems in strategic implementation-Simple, Functional, Divisional and Matrix.

STRATEGY IMPLEMENTATION

Implementation of strategy involves a number of interrelated decisions, choices, and a broad range of activities requiring a synthesis of all units, levels and members. There are two interrelated task systems involved in the process.

i. Differentiation

ii. Integration

Differentiation and Integration

The differentiation, or organizing task, is related with segmentation or division of the total strategic plan into its component parts, that is the sub-units goals and other plans of activities are to be carried out by divisions, departments and units.

In addition to the differentiation of activities and responsibilities, it is necessary that the management should coordinate and integrate diverse activities and roles into a unified, cohesive approach.

1. At the functional level of each business unit (production, marketing, etc.).
2. At the business or product level, coordinating the various business units or SBU's.
3. At the corporate level, where each of the major business plans must be integrated into a total system strategy.

Translating strategic goals into operating plans and activities is an integral part of the differentiation. Planning for implementation of strategy is defined as the process of developing goals and activities for various levels of the organization.

Resource Allocation

Decisions bearing on the allocation of resources have a vital significance in the process of strategy implementation. In a single product firm, resource allocation may involve assessment of the resource of the resource needs of different functional departments and in multi-divisional organizations; it implies assessing the resource needs of different SBU's or product divisions.

Resources may be said to consist of four broad categories:

i. Money
ii. Facilities and equipment's

iii. Materials, supplies and services

iv. Personnel

These formulate as means or instrumentalities used by an organization, to produce goods and services of value through the conversion process. The success of a company is determined by the quality of available resources, the resource conversion policy (the range of activities decided to be taken and product markets decided to be served) and the quality of decisions allocating the resources. Thus, an important aspect of strategic planning is resource planning. The first phases of resource planning consist of determining the amount and type of each resource that will be required to implement the actions and policies under the chosen strategy, and then determining the availability of each type of resource quantity during the planning period. In the second phase it must be determined whether and to what extent additional resources can be generated or acquired, and how the resource planning process should incorporate all allocation of resources that are expected to be available in accordance with the requirements of the organization units and the operative strategy of the firm.

Approaches to resource allocation

The conceptual models used for strategic choice (the growth-share matrix, stop-light and directional policy models) facilitate resource allocation in multidivisional firms. The growth-share Matrix suggests that business segments with low growth/high market share position should be allocated resources so as to maintain the present share and shifting of the cash flow generated to segments with high growth/low market share. Thus, resource allocation may be governed by considerations of competitive capabilities/market share/business strengths on the one hand, and growth prospects/industry attractiveness of business segments on the other.

A second approach is the product life cycle system of budgeting resources suggesting that resource allocation should be in accordance with the stages in the product lifecycle. The basic proposition being that resource needs vary at different stages of life cycle of a product and the strategic choice is also influenced by changes in the stage of its life cycle. For instance, with retrenchment strategy assigned to a product division, one may suggest that it would be useful to adopt a zero-based budgeting, which implies that resource allocation should rely on budget requests justified in detail from its inception and not in the light of allocation of the previous period.

SYSTEMS IN STRATEGIC IMPLEMENTATION

Growth Patterns of Large Corporations

There is a change in the structure of the organization as it grows and expands into new geographical locations and diversifies into new product markets. A new firm with a simple structure consistently experiences and increase in sales revenue and the product output over a period. It may also engage in some vertical integration to secure sources of supply (backward integration) as well as channels of distribution (forward integration). After a time, the simple-structure firm implements a functional structure to concentrate efforts to incorporate increasing efficiency and an enhancement of operations and products. The structure enables the firm to group its operations into functions, departments or geographic areas. As its initial markets mature, a firm looks beyond its present products and markets for possible expansion. Such a policy of related diversification necessitates reorganization around product lines or geographic markets leading to a divisional structure. As the business expands in terms of sales revenues, and domestic growth opportunities become limited, a firm may aspire for international markets. At this time, a firm has a wide variety of structures to choose from, including geographic area, global product division, international division, worldwide functional division and worldwide matrix. Deciding upon the most appropriate structure when a firm procures international operations depends on three primary factors:

i. Extent of international expansion

ii. Type of strategy (global, multidomestic or transnational)

iii. Degree of product diversity

There are also some other common growth patterns. For example, some firms may find it advantageous to diversify into several product lines, rather than focus on strengthening distribution and supplier relationship through vertical integration. Thus, they would organize themselves according to product lines by implementing a divisional structure. Also, some firms may choose to move into unrelated product area, typically by acquiring existing businesses. Frequently, their rationale is that acquiring assets and competencies is more economical or expedient than developing them internally. Such an unrelated or conglomerate strategy requires relatively little time internally. Such an unrelated or conglomerate strategy requires relatively little integration across business and sharing of resources. Thus, a holding company structure becomes appropriate. As we would expect, there are many other growth patterns, but the most common types of organizational structure are:

i. Simple

ii. Functional

iii. Divisional

iv. Matrix

Simple, Functional Divisional Structure and Matrix Structure

Simple structure

A simple structure is the oldest and the most common organizational form. After all, most organizations are very small and have a single or a very narrow product line. Conceding maximum over the owner manager with the work force supplementing the manager.

A simple structure is characterized by a high degree of informality. Tasks are coordinated under immediate administration with concentrated decisions lacking expertise and specificity. The performance evaluation and system of rewards is also informal rules and regulations. Usually, it is the owner who is actively involved in all the stages and departments of the business and at times a Manager may be appointed to supervise operations on a daily basis.

Such small firms with simple and straightforward structures tend to encourage creativity, and the lack of rigidity and rules also fosters individualism. However, such as an informal environment may also create problems as employees may not take their responsibilities seriously or may not comprehend them altogether. This may result in unnecessary confusion and conflicts. The absence of rigidity may encourage employees to indulge in self-interest. Such actions can erode motivation and satisfaction, as well as lead to the possible misuse or organizational resources. Further, small organizations have flat structures (i.e., few vertical, hierarchical levels) that limit opportunities for upward mobility. Without potential for future advancement, acquiring and sustaining talent may become very difficult.

Functional Structure

When an organization is small with fifteen or less employees, it is not necessary to have a variety of formal arrangements and grouping of activities. But with the steady expansion of firms, it may prove to be difficult for an owner/manager to oversee all the processes of the business and the manager may not be skilled in all the areas or tasks. He may be lacking sufficient knowledge of marketing, production, accounting and engineering to run the business on his own. Thus, specialists need to be hired in various functional areas such as growth in the overall scope and the complexity of the business further necessitates a functional structure, wherein the primary objectives and major functions of the firm are grouped internally and led by a specialist. One of the primary functions of the manager is the regulation and synthesis of the functional area.

Functional structures are most suitable for firms wherein there is just one product or a single product along with a closely-related service; the volume of production is high and there is some level of vertical integration. At first, firms tend to expand the overall scope of their operations by penetrating existing markets, introducing similar products in additional markets, or increasing the level of vertical integration. Such expansion activities clearly increase the scope and complexity of the operations. The functional structure facilitates a high level of centralization ensuring integration and control over all the related activities in the value chain-primary and support. Companies such as Videocon Industries, Hindalco and Bajaj Auto follow such a functional organization structure.

Divisional Structure

Also called the multidivisional structure, this refers to a structure that revolves around markets, projects and products. Each division has departments with their respective functional specialists. This type of a structure consists of relatively autonomous units centrally governed by a corporate office. The different divisions enjoy a fair degree of independence when dealing with their respective products and services.

In such an operational structure, there is immense responsibility on the top management with regards to decision making. Therefore, it may become essential for the top management to delegate their responsibilities and decision making powers to lower-level managers, in order to be able to attend to issues concerning the organization in the future. This makes divisional executives crucial and in conjunction with corporate-level executives, they help to determine the product market and financial objectives for the division as well as their division's contribution to the overall corporate performance.

General Motors became of the first to establish the divisional organizational structure. In the 1920s the company formed five major product divisions (Cadillac, Buick, Oldsmobile, Pontiac and Chevrolet) as well as several industrial divisions. Since then, many firms have discovered that as they diversified into new product-market activities and functional structures-with their emphasis on single functional departments-they were unable to manage the increased complexity of the entire business.

There are many advantages associated with the divisional structure. By creating separate divisions to manage individual product markets, there is a division of strategical and operational supervision. That is, divisional managers can focus their efforts on improving operations in the product markets for which they are responsible, and corporate officers can devote their time to overall strategic issues for the entire corporate offices can devote their time to overall strategic issues for the entire corporate. The focus on a division's products and markets by the divisional executives provides the corporation with an enhanced ability to respond quickly to important changes in the external environment. Since there are functional department with each division of the corporation, the difficulties of overlapping resources across department are curtailed. Finally, because there are multiple levels of general managers (that is, executives responsible for integrating and coordinating all functional areas), the development of the general management talent is enhanced.

A divisional structure also comes with potential disadvantages. First, it can be very expensive, i.e., there can be increased costs to the duplication of personnel, operations and investments. They can also be dysfunctional competition among divisions since each division tends to become concerned solely with its own operations. Furthermore, divisional managers are often evaluated on common measures such as return on assets and increasing in sales growth. Therefore, overlapping objectives can create a 'zero-sum' game curtailing shared concepts and resources amidst varying segments.

Another drawback could be that with so many divisions providing a variety of products and services, there are chances of differences arising in the quality and image of the products. There are two variations of the divisional form of organizational structure:

i. Strategic business unit (SBU) Structure

ii. Holding company structure

(i) Strategic business unit (SBU) structure

Corporations that are highly diversified, such as Unilever, may consist of dozens of different divisions. Now, if Unilever were to use a purely divisional structure, it would be nearly impossible for the corporate office to plan and coordinate activities as the span of control would be too large. Instead of attaining synergies, Unilever has put its diverse businesses into few primary SBUs.

With an SBU structure, segments with corresponding markets congregate to achieve synergy. These include related diversification, such as leveraging core competencies, sharing infrastructures and market power. Generally speaking, the more related the business are within a corporation, the fewer the SBUs required. Each of the SBUs in the corporation operates as a profit centre.

The main benefit of the SBU structure is that it simplifies the planning process aiding the corporate office to regulate and device tasks. As it facilitates decentralization of authority, distinct businesses can respond swiftly to altering conditions rather the varying segments reporting to the corporate office.

There are also some disadvantages to the SBU structure. Since the divisions are grouped into SBUs, it may become cumbersome to unite varying divisions that is, if divisions that are included in different SBUs have potential sources of synergy, it may become difficult for them to be realized. The additional level of management increases the number of personnel and overhead expenses, while the additional hierarchical level distances the corporate office further specific segments. Thus, the corporate office may become unaware of key developments that could have a major impact on the corporation.

(ii) Holding company structure

Also called a conglomerate, the holding company structure is similar to the divisional structure. While the SBU structure is used when there are obvious similarities between the individual business units (or divisions), the holding company structure is appropriated when the business in a corporation's portfolio fail to hold a common ground. Thus, the potential for synergies is limited.

Holding company structures are most appropriate for firms that follow a strategy of unrelated diversification. Companies have relied on the holding company structure to implement their unrelated diversification strategies. Since there are few similarities in businesses, the corporate offices in these companies provide enormous independence across segments rather than emphasizing on the finances and incentives proffered to increase the work output. Corporate departments are usually small, as their function across segments is limited.

The primary benefit of the holding company structure is that is cuts down cost because of fewer personnel and lower overhead, resulting from a small corporate office and fewer levels in the corporate hierarchy. Also, the autonomy motivates the heads of the divisions, inciting them to respond promptly to contingencies.

The main drawback of this structure is that corporate-level executives are not able to exercise control on the division executives. Major problems could arise if key divisional executives leave the firm, depleting the already hard press 'bench strength', owing to a lack of additional managerial talent ready to fill key positions on short notice. If problems arise in a division, it may become formidable to turn around individual business because of limited staff support in the corporate office.

Matrix Structure

Often, managers may find that it is difficult to find a suitable structure to fulfill all their requirements. If none of the approaches so far work, the managers have the option of trying the matrix structure which makes up for the drawbacks of the other structures, incorporating both functional and divisional structures.

Here, the functional departments are required to work with product groups depending on the project that requires attention. If a product group wishes to develop an additional product, it could turn to the functional departments such as engineering, marketing or production for personnel.

These personnel will assist the product group as required till the project is completed. Such borrowed personnel are answerable to their own functional heads, as well as heads of the product group they are assisting. In some multinational companies, the matrix structure helps merge product groups as well as geographical units. This is required when product managers are responsible for the global development, management and distribution of their product line; and heads of geographical regions are responsible for the profits of their business units in their respective regions.

The matrix structure is successfully used in companies such as Disney, Caterpillar Inc. and ABB. A matrix structure accredits to the benefit of specialized personnel, special equipment and facilities. Instead of duplicating functions, the resources are shared as required. Such sharing and collaboration of resources ensures efficient and effective utilization of resources. This also ensures a prompt response to changes in the competitive environment.

Another benefit is the matrix structure is flexible, providing professionals with a wide range of responsibility, giving them experience and the opportunity to develop their skills and competencies.

Matrix structures also have many drawbacks. Their dual reporting structure leads to uncertainty and conflict with regard to allocation of resources. This, in turn, causes complicated relationships at the workplace. Therefore, there is increasing reliance on group processes and teamwork. Responsibilities are diffused which may lead to delays in decisions marketing.

SUMMARY

- Implementation of strategy involves a number of interrelated decisions, choices, and a broad range of activities requiring a synthesis of all units, levels and members. There are two interrelated task systems involved in the process-Differentiation and Integration.
- Decisions bearing on the allocation of resources have a vital significance in the process of strategy implementation.
- There is a change in the structure of the organization as it grows and expands into new geographical locations and diversifies into new product markets.
- A simple structure is the oldest and most common organizational form
- Functional structures are most suitable for firms wherein there is just one product or a single product along with a closely related service.
- Divisional structure revolves around markets, projects and products.
- Matrix structure incorporates functional and divisional structures and makes up for the drawbacks of other structures.

KEY TERMS

- **Simple structure:** Oldest and most common organizational form.
- **Functional structure:** Most suitable for firms wherein there is just one product or a single product along with a closely related service.
- **Divisional structure:** Revolves around markets, projects and products.

- **Matrix structure:** Incorporates functional and divisional and divisional structures and makes up for the drawbacks of other structures.
- **Structures Business Unit (SBU):** Corporations that are highly diversified and consist of dozens of different divisions.
- **Holding company structure:** Also called conglomerate, and similar to the divisional structure.

ANSWERS TO 'CHECK YOUR PROGRESS'

1. Resources may be said to consist of four broad categories:
   i. Money
   ii. Facilities and equipment
   iii. Materials, supplies and services
   iv. Personnel
2. The most common types of organizational structures are:
   i. Simple
   ii. Functional
   iii. Divisional
   iv. Matrix
3. Two disadvantage of the divisional structure are:
   i. It can be very expensive
   ii. There can be dysfunctional competition among divisions since each division must staff multiple functional departments.
4. The primary benefit of a the holding company structure is that it cuts down cost because of fewer personnel and lower overhead, resulting from a small corporate office and fewer levels in the corporate hierarchy.

QUESTIONS AND EXPERCISES

Short –Answer Questions

1. State the three levels of integration
2. What are the three primary factors to consider when a firm procures international operations?
3. What are the two variations of the divisional form of organizational structure?
4. Write a short note on the Matrix structure?

Long- Answer Questions

1. Explain in detail strategy implementation
2. What are the different systems in strategic implementation? Elaborate.

FURTHER READING

Johnson, Gerry and Kevan Scholes. 1994. Exploring Corporate Strategy: Text and Cases. New Delhi: Prentice-Hall of India.

Thompson, Arthur A. and A.J.Strickland. 1997. Strategic Management: Concepts and Cases. Illinois: Irwin Professional Publishing.

Dess, Gregory G., G.T. Lumpkin and Alan B.Eisner. 2008. Strategic Management: Text and Cases. New York: McGraw-Hill/Irwin.

Pearce, John A. and Richard B. Robinson. 1999. Strategic Management. New York: McGraw-Hill.

Kazmi, Azhar. 2002. Business Policy and Strategic Management. New Delhi: Tata McGraw-Hill.

Unit 6

STRATEGIC CONTROL AND OPERATIONAL CONTORL

INTRODUCTION

Good operational strategies can significantly curtail the manufacturing expenditure, and also sustain the quality of the product. In this Unit, we will be looking at operational strategies used by companies. Also, there is a detailed discussion on the marking strategies- product, distribution, pricing, promotion, etc. Financial management strategy is also discussed, such as foreign exchange meaning of currency risk, exposure, currency risk management, and corporate response to exchange rate fluctuations.

UNIT OBJECTIVES

After going through this unit, you will be able to:

- Explain operational strategy
- Discuss marketing strategy
- Learn about financial management strategy

OPERATIONAL STRATEGY

Effective operational strategies can significantly curtail the manufacturing expenditure, as well as sustain the quality of the product. As discussed previously various factors are operative in operational strategies. Locations play a primary role in reducing the cost of manufacture as well as maintaining the quality standards. The location of the manufacturing facility is based on various factors like the country, the technology and the product.

It becomes significant for the manufacturing facility to be located in a country which enjoys an economic and political stability. Concerns like varying exchange rates effect the company, in case raw materials are imported and subsequently, finished goods are exported to other countries. There is a danger of a loss of cost competitiveness in case of high exchange rates. The political scenario in the country factors the investment policies. An unstable political environment may necessitate a change in the FDI policy, which determines the extent to which foreign companies can participate in domestic production activity. The infrastructure of a country too affects the location of the factory. Factors like the power supply, the telecommunication systems, and the transport facilities all affect the choice of the location. Other factors that influence the location constitute the factor costs and productivity in various countries which include labor, capital and enterprise considerations. A Return on Investment (ROI) depends on these factors and thus, land and labor are significant in determining the location of the manufacturing facility.

The manufacturing technology also determines the number of locations for the manufacturing facility. If the technology entails a high expenditure then the locations of the manufacturing plant will be few. Economies of scale are also operative in the location factor, which involves the reduction in the per-unit cost of production due to an increase in the scale of operation. Customization of products results in an increase in the cost and thus, standardization was considered increasingly cost-effective but in industries like the automobile, customization acquires a greater relevance as it provides the flexibility to alter designs, in accordance to the market responses. The value-to-weight ratio and the nature of the need of the product affect the product, which in turn also determines the location of the plant.

Companies can either opt for producing or purchasing different units. Sourcing of segments from outside can curtail financial and operational risks and curb down the cost of labor, plant and machinery. This can also be advantageous as sourcing can provide an opportunity to utilize various manufacturers superior technology. For example, Sundaram Clayton in India specializes in manufacturing radiator caps. It has been awarded the Deming Prize for quality in this item. Rather than investing in the production of this item, automobile manufacturers worldwide prefer to source radiator caps from Sundaram Clayton since it makes them most efficiently. The primary drawback of outsourcing is the increasing supplier dependency it entails. Production delays on the supplier's end can result in heavy delays and expenditure. Many businesses have been integrated due to outsourcing. There are three kinds of integration namely, forward, backward and horizontal integration.

To generate economies of scale and reduce the risk of dependence on suppliers, for example, Ford established plants that specialize in a single component, say, air conditioners and supplies them to other locations for the final assembling of cars. Similarly, Airbus Industries, the aircraft manufacturer source components form numerous locations across Europe and performs the final assembling of aircraft in France and Germany. An alternative to investment in in-house manufacturing of components is for the company to hold equity in the suppliers' firms, giving the company effective control over the cost, reliability and quality of supplies.

Logistics management essentially constitutes that part of a supply chain which plans, implements and controls the efficient transportation of goods and services. Various complications of goods transport including differing time-zones, transport modes and infrastructural facilities and regulatory laws impede an efficient transport of goods.

Logistics is a strategic, not an operational decision since it involves careful planning and has cross-functional applicability, and since the decision impacts the value of the firm as a result of savings in cost. Moreover, the amount and nature of materials and components, packaging, storage and distribution infrastructure requirements can affect the design of the product.

Supply chain management is a more comprehensive function than logistics management. It integrates the activities of demand forecasting, procurement, manufacture, distribution and inventory management. MNC with manufacturing facilities in several countries use Logistics Information Systems (LIS) to reduce delivery time and inventory costs. The challenge of SCM is to mitigate the bull-whip effect. The bull-whip effect is the distortion of actual demand information that occurs as a company moves further away from its customers.

SCM is facilitated by the use of the Internet. Networking tools that connect individual customers and suppliers or provides e-commerce portals have helped improve the information flow between the buyer and supplier thereby strengthening SCM. SCM, in turn, has helped boost the growth of e-commerce transactions. Enterprise Resource Planning (ERP) helps in connecting suppliers and buyers and helps in managing manufacture, inventory and quality. The widely acclaimed procurement mechanism of Wal-Mart, USA, is an example of the growing partnership between suppliers and buyers.

MARKETING STRATEGY

Strategies for marketing must take into consideration different aspects of product, pricing, distribution and promotion.

Product

A product may be considered as a set of attributes. A firm should take account of all the major attributes of its products. But all the attributes may not be assigned equal importance in all the markets. Consumers in different countries may want different features according to their economic and cultural environments.

Cultural differences

According to some management experts, consumers' tastes around the world are converging due to the revolution in technology that has improved the scope and speed of communication, transport and travel. The global acceptance of McDonald's burgers, Coca-Cola, MTV programmes and Levi's jeans are indications of convergence of tastes.

However, culture still has a significant bearing on consumer behavior, which in turn, affects the marketing environment. Taste in food varies from culture to culture. Hot spicy foods are popular in many Asian countries; less spicy food is popular in America. Pork consumption is forbidden in Islamic countries. The interpretation of colours is also significantly different. While white is associated with purity and cleanliness in the west, it signifies death in Asian countries. Sometimes, cultural differences may arise for historical reasons.

Economic differences

Consumer disposable income also influences the purchasing decisions of customers. The marketability of luxury cars, convenience goods, etc., in developing countries suggests that most consumer products have a universal market. People would like to buy them if they can afford them.

In emerging markets like china, India, Brazil, Indonesia, Mexico, etc., business risks are high but there is a huge potential market. Though the role of marketing in low-income countries is the same as in high income countries, the focus is different. Market research and marketing have to identify and respond to people's needs and wants appropriately. People in low-income countries are likely to attach importance to basic attributes and low process, while people in developed countries demand additional attributes even if prices go up. In the US, the high-income levels, large distances, low cost of petrol, and lifestyle factors (e.g. spending more time outdoors), all lead to greater demand for additional luxuries and comforts in cars. The demand for sports utility vehicles (SUVs) is high in the US, but negligible in the developing countries like India. Affordability is the prime consideration, followed by fuel efficiency and product durability, in developing markets. For example, in India, four-stroke bikes compete more on mileage than on any other performance attribute.

In Japan, though the standard of living is high, people prefer small appliances that fit into their small houses and consume less electricity.

Technical standards

Products designed for one country may not be appropriate for another country due to the differences in technical standards. In the 1950s and 1960s, different countries in Asia have different technical standards for television signal frequency. Therefore, television and video equipment had to be customized. When companies failed to adhere to these standards, their television did not sell.

Distribution

Distribution refers to the choice of the mode of delivery of products to the customer. It is a crucial part of a MNC's marketing mix and may vary from country to country.

Typical distribution system

In a typical distribution system, there are two tiers between the manufacturer and the final consumer- the wholesale distributor and the retailer. If the manufacturer is outside the country, the product may be sold to an export agency, which then supplies the product to the wholesaler. A distribution channel could have additional tiers or fewer tiers than this. An MNC may sell directly to wholesale distributors or retailers or even to consumers in some countries, whereas in other countries it may employ a lengthier channel.

Differences in distribution channels in different countries: Retail system

The retail system in some countries is highly concentrated, while in others, it is extremely fragmented. In a fragmented system, no one particular retailer caters to a significant fraction of the market. When the system is concentrated, a small number of retailers serve a majority of the consumers. In the US and Germany, a small number of retail chains control most of the market for food products and groceries. In India, retail distribution is highly fragmented and no particular chain caters to a significant percentage of the market. While one of the reasons for the differences in retail system is the level of economic development, history and tradition may also contribute to the differences in retail systems. In many developed countries, people shop only on weekends. To serve such customers, large shopping malls with several facilities are located at places where customers can park their cars and shop in comfort. The retail outlet concentration is high in these countries, whereas retail outlets are highly dispersed in countries like China, Japan and India, where lifestyles are different.

Channel length

Channel length refers to the number of individual entities between the producer and the final consumer of the product. If a firm sells its product directly to the consumer, the channel length is less, i.e., there is only the producer and the consumer. If the product passes through intermediaries like the import agent, wholesaler and retailer before reaching the customer, the channel is long. The choice of channel is a strategic decision for the firm. The firm's decision depends on the type of retail system in the country. In a country where the retail system is highly fragmented, firms cannot afford to make sales calls to each retailer. Firms, therefore, prefer to deal with a few wholesalers rather than employ a huge sales force to supply to widely scattered retailers.

Channel accessibility

This refers to the ease with which a new firm can access shelf space in the retail outlets of a country. Sometimes, manufactures and distributors have long-standing trading relationships.

Sometimes, a manufacturer promises attractive margins to a distributor who doesn't stock a competitors' product. Such agreements are common in Japan, making it difficult for foreign firms to gain access to distribution channels.

Choosing a distribution strategy: The firm may choose a short or long channel depending on the relative costs and benefits of each. A firm's decision to choose a distribution strategy is based on three factors-type of retailing system, channel length and channel accessibility.

Choosing a distributor: An MNC should follow a well-designed strategy to penetrate markets, particularly in emerging markets. An MNC hires local distributors, as it is not familiar with local markets and business practices. The MNCs should be able to anticipate potential problems in distribution and take steps to avoid them. The distributor may not invest in expanding his business because of lack of funds or for other reasons.

An MNC should assess potential markets and identify the right distributor rather than waiting for a distributor to approach it with a proposal. An MNC may select a distributor on the basis of market surveys indicating the preferred suppliers of a majority of the retailers.

Though the major concern of an MNC when it enters an emerging market is to select distributors and to acquire a customer base, it should also work on developing a network among its distributors within a country. It may also work on developing a network among distributors within a county. It may also encourage distributors to form an association to exchange ideas, product plans and designs. This brings about consistency in products manufactured by national licenses, customization for local markets and economies of scales.

Pricing

An MNC has to consider a wide range of factors when determining the price of a product. Product-specific, market-specific and environmental factors influence international pricing. Further, price setting is also influenced at three levels- the internal level, the macro level and the micro level. At the internal level, the firm is concerned about the return on investment, sales volume and costs. The price should cover the costs of producing and marketing the product in different countries. At the same time, the price should not exceed the perceived value of the product.

At the macro level, government restrictions influence international pricing. The business cycle stage, exchange rate and cultural factors also influence pricing decisions. For example, firms have to depend on competitive pricing strategies in China as the market has just entered the growth stage of its life cycle. The internal and macro levels together influence the international pricing of a product in the microenvironment, i.e., at the industry level. An MNC should take into account the following factors before pricing its products in different countries.

Competitive structure

The competitor's prices have to be carefully evaluated before setting prices. The level of competition in the country depends on the stage of the product's life cycle of the country.

Price discrimination

Products can be positioned as premium products in one country and as low-price products in another. Heineken markets its beers in some countries at the average market price, while in several other countries; it uses the premium price strategy. The difference is mainly due to the differences in the price structure of various countries.

Distribution Structure

The structure of the distribution network is also a major determinant of pricing policy. The structure varies in different countries depending on the relative power of buyers and suppliers. In some countries, suppliers may dominate and have the power to determine price, while in others buyers may have more influence on prices. For example, the distribution structure of the frozen ready meal market in Germany is a major determinant of pricing.

Consumer behavior

Consumer perception of the quality of a product is an important element in pricing. In India, most purchasing decisions are extremely sensitive to the price of the product. Marketers of food products, toilet soaps, cleaning powders, consumer electronics, etc., get a very positive in terms of sales generated when they offer discounts. In contrast, particularly for food products, in developed countries, demand in less price-sensitive as food takes up a very small proportion of the income of individuals. For consumer electronics too, people in developed countries may not respond as positively to price reductions, since in many cases, it is old stock that are discounted in this fashion.

Strategic pricing

MNCs have to adapt their pricing according to the country's preferences. The Italian automobile market has no room for imported cars positioned on price because of the presence of low-cost domestic manufacturer, Fiat. Fiat's competitive advantage lies in its ability to manufacture cheap cars for price-sensitive consumers in Latin America and North Africa. Fiat's cost leadership strategy acts as an entry barrier.

Government policies, subsidies and regulations also influence pricing strategies. The high excise duties on liquor in some countries like Australia and India compel liquor producers to set high prices of profitability.

From a strategic perspective, the success and survival of a company depends on its understanding of the differences in the countries in terms of price structure, distribution structure and consumer behavior. The company's management has to identify, appreciate and accommodate these differences in order to use price as a strategic tool.

Promotion

MNCs should not only have a clear understanding of how to position their product but also should be able to communicate well with prospective customers. For effective promotion, MNCs need to choose an appropriate channel-direct selling, sales promotion, direct marketing, advertising in different media, or a combination of two or more of these. The choice of communication strategy is determined by various factors such as cultural differences, customer awareness, lifestyles, etc.

Barriers to International Communication

Cultural differences can pose considerable complications in international communication. A message appropriate in one country may be considered inappropriate in another, marketing the company's reputation in a country. To avoid this, local agencies are employed to restructure the message retaining the inherent meaning of the message including a local aspect in the ad. Recruiting a local sales force and training sales personnel in local languages facilitates direct sales.

Pull vs push strategy

Pricing and Product availability are major factors that affect sale. A push strategy primarily deals with the incorporation of a large sales force for personal selling entailing high costs. A pull strategy constitutes intensive advertising to create a demand drawing customers. Push and pull strategies are operated in tandem to increase the effectiveness of communication. Other factors including customer awareness, channel length and media availability have a prominent impact on the development of a firm's business strategy.

Customer awareness

Creating customer awareness becomes primary in the operation of a pull strategy. As the costs are relatively low, the target audience needs to be large. The expenditure entailed is significantly higher in comparison to advertising in the mass media, but direct selling is effective for products where consumer awareness is low. Eureka Forbes has been successful in introducing vacuum cleaners in India through the incorporation of this strategy. Direct-door-to-door sale techniques were effective in producing desired results.

Length of the Channel

The channel is proportionate to the intermediaries involved in the process of product transportation. It becomes quite cumbersome to influence the intermediaries at each level. Multiple levels in the distribution channels require intensive adverting of create demand, which facilitates availability of distributors.

Media internationally

Different forms of advertising (Comparative, direct, aggressive, defensive etc.) are employed to convey varying messages to prospective customers. The content of the advertisement is significant in the formation of the product's public perception. Product categories fall under different usages in varying countries and thus advertisements need to be adapted accordingly. For example: in the US motorcycles constitute a recreational category, while in South Asia motorcycles are key instruments of transportation.

Configuring the marketing mix

The configuration of a marketing mix may vary from country to country based on economic, social and cultural factors as well as, competitive conditions, technical standard, distribution network and government regulations. The production and distribution strategy of a product may vary in keeping with these distinctions. Although a standardization of the marketing mix can substantially cut down on the expenditure, it is significant to customize for effective sale. Thus, a similitude needs to be maintained between the extent to customization and standardization.

FINANCIAL MANAGEMENT STRATEGY

Currency risk is one of the unique problems faced by the internationally operating firms. Currency risk can be managed taking a short-term view and using financial instruments to hedge against specific risks. A long-term strategy of diversifying across products, markets and suppliers might involve more initial investment, but subsequently lower short-term hedging costs.

Foreign Exchange

In a foreign exchange market, individual's banks and other institutions trade in currencies. The principle purpose of a foreign exchange market is to allow traders to have access to foreign currencies required for the export and import of goods and services. At present foreign exchange markets around the world are equipped with efficient information systems and access to the global Clearing House Inter-bank Payment System (CHIPs), which makes international financial transactions effective and smooth.

The price of one currency in terms of another is called exchange rate. It is determined by factors affecting the demand and supply of the currency in the foreign exchange market. Changes and fluctuations in the exchange rate can be destabilizing. Therefore analysts try to predict exchange rates on the basis of anticipated demand and supply. Ways have also been devised to minimize the problems that arise due to fluctuations in exchange rates, as given below-

Cash, Tom, Spot and Forward Rates

Cash is the defined as the exchange rate for currencies to be delivered immediately or in the same day. Tom is the rate currencies a day after the day of contract. Sport rate is the exchange rate for currencies to be delivered 2 days after the day of the contract. Forward rates are exchange rates for currencies to be delivered later. There are many forward delivery dates, one-month forward, three-month forward, six-month forward, etc. These rates depict the market's view about the movement likely to occur in the currency. Forward rates are expressed in terms of percentages.

Bid- ask spreads

These are quotations of price (exchange rate) between dealers in foreign exchange. Bid is the price at which one dealer will buy the currency in exchange for another currency. Ask is the price at which the dealer will sell the currency. The bid price slightly lower than the ask price. The Bid- Ask difference is called the spread and it is the profit in the transaction for the dealer. A higher spread indicates less trading in the currency. A very low spread is an indication of high liquidity in the markets for the currency.

Arbitrage

Riskless profit made by buying and selling the same securities in two different markets simultaneously, is termed as arbitrage. Arbitrage opportunities exit when there is mis-pricing of the instruments in the two markets.

Meaning of Currency Risk

The exchange rate has a direct bearing on the business of the company. Let us suppose GM Chevrolet cars are priced at USD 30,000. The exchange rate is 45 Rs/$. So an India importer will have to pay Rs1, 35,000 (30000*45), excluding other costs. If the rupee falls to 46/$, importer will have to pay Rs 1,380,000 (30000*46). But if the rupee appreciates to 44/$ then the importer will have to pay Rs 1,320,000 (30000*44).

Exposure: Meaning and Types

The sensitivity of a firm's cash flow to changes in exchange rates is called exposure. Such exposure can be long term short terms of only of an accounting nature. Hedging (protecting) instruments and strategies for managing these exposures are discussed later on in the Unit.

Economic exposure

This refers to the long-term outlook of the company's investments that are already made or are likely to be made in a country. This exposure is difficult to assess as it involves a subjective projection of future cash flows. Measurement and management of economic exposure requires a long-term strategic plan, influencing the overall value of the firm.

Transaction exposure

This is similar to economic exposure except that it adds for a shorter term. Transaction exposure is caused by any likely change in future cash flows due to changes in exchange rates after completion of transactions but before the actual receipt of cash. There are various strategies for Hedging (Protecting) against such exposure.

Translation exposure

Translation exposure arises on the basis of Accounting for transactions between trading companies. The holding company in a country needs to include the accounts of its subsidiary in its balance sheet. Investors across the world will require the balance sheet to be in the currency of the country to which the holding company belongs. US GAAP defines translation exposure arising out of changes in the value of net monetary assets. "Net monetary assets" is the difference between monetary assets and liabilities. Monetary assets include cash, receivables and stock and monetary liabilities include payables and long-term debt.

Currency Risk Management Alternatives

The liberalization of government regulations regarding international movement of capital and financial and technological innovation has made currency risk management simpler and more accurate. Derivative instruments were developed initially to protect merchandise traders from fluctuations in the prices of commodities. But their application is being rapidly extended to fund management, HR policies and enterprise-wide risk management.

Derivative instruments and their uses

Constitute agreements pertain to the purchase or sale of a product at an impeding date, at a consented price. These contracts primarily keep a check on the fluctuating prices removing the uncertainty of unstable prices.

A standardized form of forward contracts, these are binding contracts for a future exchange of a commodity on a stated date, at a specified price. However, these contracts are directed through an exchange authorized for this transaction. The exchange deals with issues like the size of contacts. The delivery dates, as well as the acquisition of deposit margins form the contracting parties reducing the default risk, which is warranted to the exchange.

Corporate Response to Exchange Rate Fluctuations

Forecasting exchange rates

Forecasting exchange rates is a primary role of a corporate finance manager. Many corporations like Goldman Sachs, Citibank and Wharton Forecasting Services provide forecasts on various economic indicators including exchange rates. There is no single best model for forecasting exchange rates. And no model can hold good for all time. The models used for forecasting exchange rates can be classified into two types:

(a) Fundamental Analysis Models

These models make use of economic fundamentals such as inflation rates and interest rates, and based on the established relationship between these fundamentals, exchange rates are predicted. Some more complex models use, not one, but many of these relationships to predict exchange rates.

(b) Technical Analysis Models

These models make use the historical movements in exchange rates of the countries and predict exchange rates with the use of time-series analysis and charts. It should be remembered that technical analysis provides only the direction of change and not the magnitude of change in exchange rates.

SUMMARY

- Effective operational strategies can significantly curtail the manufacturing expenditure, as well as sustain the quality of the product.
- Strategies for marketing must take into consideration different aspect of product, pricing, distribution and promotion.
- The structure of the distribution network is a major determinant of pricing policy. The structure varies in different countries depending on the relative power of buyers and suppliers.
- MNCs should not only have a clear understanding of how to position their product but also should be able to communicate well with prospective customers.
- Currency risk is one of the unique problems faced by the internationally operating firms.

KEY TERMS

- **Logistics:** Strategic decision involving careful planning and having cross-functional applicability.
- **Product:** A set of attributes. A firm should take account of all the major attributes of its products.

- **Distribution:** Refers to the choice of the mode of delivery of products to the customer
- **Channel accessibility:** refers to the ease with which a new firm can access shelf space in the retail outlets of a county.
- **Foreign exchange:** Here, market, individuals, banks and other institutions trade in different currencies.

ANSWERS TO 'CHECK YOUR PROGRESS'

1. A product may be considered as a set of attributes. A firm should take account of all the major attributes of its products.
2. Four forms of advertisement are:
   i. Comparative
   ii. Direct
   iii. Aggressive
   iv. Defensive
3. Translation exposure arises on the basis of accounting for transactions between trading companies
4. The two types of models used for forecasting exchange rates can be classified into two types:
   i. Fundamental Analysis Models
   ii. Technical Analysis Models

QUESTIONAL AND EXPERCIES

Short-Answer Questions

1. Write a short note on the influence of cultural difference on products.
2. What is a typical distribution system?
3. Write a short note on the influence of pricing on distribution.
4. List the barriers to international communication.
5. What are currency risk management alternatives?

Long-Answer Questions

1. Explain in detail operational strategy
2. What is marketing strategy? Elaborate.
3. What is financial management strategy? Explain in detail.
4. Analyse the currency risk management alternatives.

FURTHER READING

Johnson,Gerry and Kevan Scholes. 1994. Exploring Corporate Strategy: Text and Cases. New Delhi: Prentice-Hall of India.

Thompson, Arthur A. and A.J.Strickland. 1997. Strategic Management: Concepts and Cases. Illinois: Irwin Professional Publishing.

Dess, Gregory G., G.T. Lumpkin and Alan B.Eisner. 2008. Strategic Management: Text and Cases. New York: McGraw-Hill/Irwin.

Pearce, John A. and Richard B. Robinson. 1999. Strategic Management. New York: McGraw-Hill.

Kazmi, Azhar. 2002. Business Policy and Strategic Management. New Delhi: Tata McGraw-Hill.

ABOUT THE AUTHOR

Dr Mysore Ambashankar is the Dean and Director - Academics of Gupta College of Management and Technology, Bangalore specializing in Corporate Strategy, Organizational Behavior and Marketing apart from other management subjects. Prof M Ambashankar is an Engineering Professional and has to his credit PhD and DSc in Management and Organizational Psychology respectively. Has more than three decades of combined experience in Corporates and in Academia and this expertise helps students to understand complex concepts and applications with ease. Prof M Ambashankar has published few hundred articles in academic journals and also has published peer-reviewed scholarly research work in International Magazines. He serves on the Boards of several academic Institutions in the capacity of Adviser and also a visiting Professor at South Pacific Universities and also an in-house faculty for TQM for fortune 500 organizations. Prof M Ambashankar teaches MBA and International MBA programs at various renowned Business Schools in India and overseas and has received awards for teaching excellence and for mentoring in both the Programs. He brings into the classroom his experience of doing business across the globe. He is a native of Mysore and presently stays in Bangalore.